Wilderness is the raw material out of which man has hammered the artifact called civilization.

No living man will see again the long-grass prairie, where a sea of prairie flowers lapped at the stirrups of the pioneer . . .

No living man will see again the virgin pineries of the Lake States, or the flat-woods of the coastal plain, or the giant hardwoods . . .

First published in 1949, Aldo Leopold's *A Sand County Almanac* is now an established environmental classic. Beginning with a beautifully written description of the seasonal changes in nature and their effect on the delicate ecological balance, the book proceeds to examples of man's destructive interference and concludes with a plea for a Wilderness esthetic which is even more urgent and timely today.

A SAND COUNTY ALMANAC

With Essays on Conservation from Round River

ALDO LEOPOLD

Illustrated by Charles W. Schwartz

A SIERRA CLUB/BALLANTINE BOOK
NEW YORK

GRATEFUL ACKNOWLEDGMENT is made to the editors of the following magazines and journals who have kindly allowed to be reprinted in book form portions or all of individual articles: *American Forests*, 'Marshland Elegy,' 'The Green Lagoons,' and 'Flambeau'; *Audubon Magazine*, 'Odyssey'; *Bird Lore*, 'Conservation Esthetic'; *The Condor*, 'The Thick Billed Parrot of Chihuahua'; *Journal of Forestry*, 'The Conservation Ethic'; *Journal of Wildlife Management*, 'Wildlife in American Culture' and 'Song of the Gavilan'; *The Land*, 'Cheat Takes Over'; *Outdoor America*, 'The Alder Fork'; *Silent Wings*, 'On a Monument to the Pigeon'; *Wisconsin Agriculturist and Farmer*, 'Bur Oak' and 'Sky Dance'; *Wisconsin Conservation Bulletin*, 'A Mighty Fortress,' 'Home Range,' and 'Pines above the Snow.' Thanks are also due to The Macmillan Company for permission to quote from 'Tristram,' copyright 1927 by Edward Arlington Robinson, on page 239.

Library of Congress Catalog Card Number: 66-28871

SBN 345-22007-2-095

This edition published by arrangement with The Oxford University Press.

First Printing: September, 1970
Second Printing: June, 1971
Third Printing: November, 1971
Fourth Printing: September, 1972
Fifth Printing: March, 1973
Sixth Printing: August, 1973

Cover photograph by Ray Atkeson

Printed in the United States of America

SIERRA CLUB
1050 Mills Tower
San Francisco, Calif. 94104

BALLANTINE BOOKS, INC.
201 East 50th Street, New York, N.Y. 10022

To my ESTELLA

Contents

Contents

A Sand County ALMANAC

Preface to the Enlarged Edition

A Sand County Almanac was in draft form when Aldo Leopold died in 1948. His son Luna edited this material and saw it through to publication in 1949. He later prepared for publication another group of previously unpublished essays and journals, these appearing in 1953 under the title *Round River*.

This new volume combines all of *Sand County Almanac* with eight essays from *Round River*. The arrangement of the essays has been somewhat altered, and in one instance two essays have been combined, in order to avoid repetition and to present Aldo Leopold's central ideas in meaningful relationship to one another. Because of this rearrangement the Foreword to the original edition no longer describes the sections as they appear in this book: Part II has been renamed, Part III has become Part IV, and a new Part III, made up mostly of essays from *Round River*, has been introduced. We have also made minor revisions

in the text itself where dated references served only
to distract the reader.

*   *   *

Though these essays have been widely read and
quoted, their basic tenets have been all but forgotten
in the glare of great national publicity extolling the
virtues of 'natural beauty.' Roadside beautification is
a far cry from the harmony between man and land
that Aldo Leopold knew and taught. The America
that declares the preservation of natural beauty to be
public policy is at the same time planning to build
dams in two areas of great natural value. Bills are
now before Congress to construct power dams in the
Grand Canyon of the Colorado that would essentially
kill the living river and flood a large part of this unique
natural heritage.

There also has been under consideration for some
years the construction of a dam for the development
of hydroelectric power in Alaska at a location that
would flood out a large portion of the breeding areas
of the migratory waterfowl of the Pacific Coast. The
construction of Rampart Dam could, in a moment of
time, eliminate most of the ducks, geese, and other
birds that each year for eons have passed over Washington, Oregon, and California. When Aldo Leopold
wrote 'Goose Music,' this could scarcely be imagined:
now this possibility is upon us. The shame is that the
Americans proposing, agreeing to, and carrying out
this plan will defend their action on financial grounds,
when economics should not be the deciding factor,
especially as alternative and feasible sources of electric power can be found.

*   *   *

This generation of Aldo Leopold's grandchildren is rebelling on college campuses, demonstrating and working for social causes, and fighting on foreign soil. This same youth is maturing at that moment of time which is pivotal in the struggle to preserve 'things wild and free' that Aldo Leopold understood so wisely and expressed so eloquently.

Of all the causes that attract the attention of these young people, the plight of nature is one which may be truly a last call. Things wild and free are being destroyed by the impersonality of our attitude toward the land. What better way to fight the destruction of nature than to place in the hands of the young this powerful plea for a land ethic?

> *Carolyn Clugston Leopold*
> *Luna B. Leopold*

Washington, D.C.
June 1966

Foreword to Sand County Almanac

THERE ARE some who can live without wild things, and some who cannot. These essays are the delights and dilemmas of one who cannot.

Like winds and sunsets, wild things were taken for granted until progress began to do away with them. Now we face the question whether a still higher 'standard of living' is worth its cost in things natural, wild, and free. For us of the minority, the opportunity to see geese is more important than television, and the chance to find a pasque-flower is a right as inalienable as free speech.

These wild things, I admit, had little human value until mechanization assured us of a good breakfast, and until science disclosed the drama of where they come from and how they live. The whole conflict thus boils down to a question of degree. We of the minority see a law of diminishing returns in progress; our opponents do not.

*   *   *

One must make shift with things as they are. These essays are my shifts. They are grouped in three parts.

Part I tells what my family sees and does at its week-end refuge from too much modernity: 'the shack.' On this sand farm in Wisconsin, first worn out and then abandoned by our bigger-and-better society, we try to rebuild, with shovel and axe, what we are losing elsewhere. It is here that we seek—and still find—our meat from God.

These shack sketches are arranged seasonally as a 'Sand County Almanac.'

Part II, 'Sketches Here and There,' recounts some of the episodes in my life that taught me, gradually and sometimes painfully, that the company is out of step. These episodes, scattered over the continent and through forty years of time, present a fair sample of the issues that bear the collective label: conservation.

Part III, 'The Upshot,' sets forth, in more logical terms, some of the ideas whereby we dissenters rationalize our dissent. Only the very sympathetic reader will wish to wrestle with the philosophical questions of Part III. I suppose it may be said that these essays tell the company how it may get back in step.

*   *   *

Conservation is getting nowhere because it is incompatible with our Abrahamic concept of land. We abuse land because we regard it as a commodity belonging to us. When we see land as a community to which we belong, we may begin to use it with love and respect. There is no other way for land to survive the impact of mechanized man, nor for us to reap from it the esthetic harvest it is capable, under science, of contributing to culture.

That land is a community is the basic concept of ecology, but that land is to be loved and respected is an extension of ethics. That land yields a cultural harvest is a fact long known, but latterly often forgotten.

These essays attempt to weld these three concepts.

Such a view of land and people is, of course, subject to the blurs and distortions of personal experience and personal bias. But wherever the truth may lie, this much is crystal-clear: our bigger-and-better society is now like a hypochondriac, so obsessed with its own economic health as to have lost the capacity to remain healthy. The whole world is so greedy for more bathtubs that it has lost the stability necessary to build them, or even to turn off the tap. Nothing could be more salutary at this stage than a little healthy contempt for a plethora of material blessings.

Perhaps such a shift of values can be achieved by reappraising things unnatural, tame, and confined in terms of things natural, wild, and free.

ALDO LEOPOLD

Madison, Wisconsin
4 March 1948

Part I

A Sand County Almanac

January

January Thaw

EACH YEAR, after the midwinter blizzards, there comes a night of thaw when the tinkle of dripping water is heard in the land. It brings strange stirrings, not only to creatures abed for the night, but to some who have been asleep for the winter. The hibernating skunk, curled up in his deep den, uncurls himself and ventures forth to prowl the wet world, dragging his belly in the snow. His track marks one of the earliest datable events in that cycle of beginnings and ceasings which we call a year.

The track is likely to display an indifference to mundane affairs uncommon at other seasons; it leads straight across-country, as if its maker had hitched his wagon to a star and dropped the reins. I follow, curious to deduce his state of mind and appetite, and destination if any.

*   *   *

3

The months of the year, from January up to June, are a geometric progression in the abundance of distractions. In January one may follow a skunk track, or search for bands on the chickadees, or see what young pines the deer have browsed, or what muskrat houses the mink have dug, with only an occasional and mild digression into other doings. January observation can be almost as simple and peaceful as snow, and almost as continuous as cold. There is time not only to see who has done what, but to speculate why.

*   *   *

A meadow mouse, startled by my approach, darts damply across the skunk track. Why is he abroad in daylight? Probably because he feels grieved about the thaw. Today his maze of secret tunnels, laboriously chewed through the matted grass under the snow, are tunnels no more, but only paths exposed to public view and ridicule. Indeed the thawing sun has mocked the basic premises of the microtine economic system!

The mouse is a sober citizen who knows that grass grows in order that mice may store it as underground haystacks, and that snow falls in order that mice may build subways from stack to stack: supply, demand, and transport all neatly organized. To the mouse, snow means freedom from want and fear.

*   *   *

A rough-legged hawk comes sailing over the meadow ahead. Now he stops, hovers like a kingfisher, and then drops like a feathered bomb into the marsh. He does not rise again, so I am sure he has caught, and is now eating, some worried mouse-engineer who could not wait until night to inspect the damage to his well-ordered world.

The rough-leg has no opinion why grass grows, but he is well aware that snow melts in order that hawks may again catch mice. He came down out of the Arctic in the hope of thaws, for to him a thaw means freedom from want and fear.

*   *   *

The skunk track enters the woods, and crosses a glade where the rabbits have packed down the snow with their tracks, and mottled it with pinkish urinations. Newly exposed oak seedlings have paid for the thaw with their newly barked stems. Tufts of rabbit-hair bespeak the year's first battles among the amorous bucks. Further on I find a bloody spot, encircled by a wide-sweeping arc of owl's wings. To this rabbit the thaw brought freedom from want, but also a reckless abandonment of fear. The owl has reminded him that thoughts of spring are no substitute for caution.

*   *   *

The skunk track leads on, showing no interest in possible food, and no concern over the rompings or retributions of his neighbors. I wonder what he has on his mind; what got him out of bed? Can one impute romantic motives to this corpulent fellow, dragging his ample beltline through the slush? Finally the track enters a pile of driftwood, and does not emerge. I hear the tinkle of dripping water among the logs, and I fancy the skunk hears it too. I turn homeward, still wondering.

February

Good Oak

THERE ARE two spiritual dangers in not owning
a farm. One is the danger of supposing that breakfast
comes from the grocery, and the other that heat
comes from the furnace.

To avoid the first danger, one should plant a garden, preferably where there is no grocer to confuse
the issue.

To avoid the second, he should lay a split of good
oak on the andirons, preferably where there is no
furnace, and let it warm his shins while a February

blizzard tosses the trees outside. If one has cut, split, hauled, and piled his own good oak, and let his mind work the while, he will remember much about where the heat comes from, and with a wealth of detail denied to those who spend the week end in town astride a radiator.

*   *   *

The particular oak now aglow on my andirons grew on the bank of the old emigrant road where it climbs the sandhill. The stump, which I measured upon felling the tree, has a diameter of 30 inches. It shows 80 growth rings, hence the seedling from which it originated must have laid its first ring of wood in 1865, at the end of the Civil War. But I know from the history of present seedlings that no oak grows above the reach of rabbits without a decade or more of getting girdled each winter, and re-sprouting during the following summer. Indeed, it is all too clear that every surviving oak is the product either of rabbit negligence or of rabbit scarcity. Some day some patient botanist will draw a frequency curve of oak birth-years, and show that the curve humps every ten years, each hump originating from a low in the ten-year rabbit cycle. (A fauna and flora, by this very process of perpetual battle within and among species, achieve collective immortality.)

It is likely, then, that a low in rabbits occurred in the middle 'sixties, when my oak began to lay on annual rings, but that the acorn that produced it fell during the preceding decade, when the covered wagons were still passing over my road into the

Great Northwest. It may have been the wash and wear of the emigrant traffic that bared this roadbank, and thus enabled this particular acorn to spread its first leaves to the sun. Only one acorn in a thousand ever grew large enough to fight rabbits; the rest were drowned at birth in the prairie sea.

It is a warming thought that this one wasn't, and thus lived to garner eighty years of June sun. It is this sunlight that is now being released, through the intervention of my axe and saw, to warm my shack and my spirit through eighty gusts of blizzard. And with each gust a wisp of smoke from my chimney bears witness, to whomsoever it may concern, that the sun did not shine in vain.

My dog does not care where heat comes from, but he cares ardently that it come, and soon. Indeed he considers my ability to make it come as something magical, for when I rise in the cold black pre-dawn and kneel shivering by the hearth making a fire, he pushes himself blandly between me and the kindling splits I have laid on the ashes, and I must touch a match to them by poking it between his legs. Such faith, I suppose, is the kind that moves mountains.

It was a bolt of lightning that put an end to wood-making by this particular oak. We were all awakened, one night in July, by the thunderous crash; we realized that the bolt must have hit near by, but, since it had not hit us, we all went back to sleep. Man brings all things to the test of himself, and this is notably true of lightning.

Next morning, as we strolled over the sandhill rejoicing with the cone-flowers and the prairie clovers over their fresh accession of rain, we came upon a

great slab of bark freshly torn from the trunk of the roadside oak. The trunk showed a long spiral scar of barkless sapwood, a foot wide and not yet yellowed by the sun. By the next day the leaves had wilted, and we knew that the lightning had bequeathed to us three cords of prospective fuel wood.

We mourned the loss of the old tree, but knew that a dozen of its progeny standing straight and stalwart on the sands had already taken over its job of wood-making.

We let the dead veteran season for a year in the sun it could no longer use, and then on a crisp winter's day we laid a newly filed saw to its bastioned base. Fragrant little chips of history spewed from the saw cut, and accumulated on the snow before each kneeling sawyer. We sensed that these two piles of sawdust were something more than wood: that they were the integrated transect of a century; that our saw was biting its way, stroke by stroke, decade by decade, into the chronology of a lifetime, written in concentric annual rings of good oak.

* * *

It took only a dozen pulls of the saw to transect the few years of our ownership, during which we had learned to love and cherish this farm. Abruptly we began to cut the years of our predecessor the bootlegger, who hated this farm, skinned it of residual fertility, burned its farmhouse, threw it back into the lap of the County (with delinquent taxes to boot), and then disappeared among the landless anonymities of the Great Depression. Yet the oak had laid down good wood for him; his sawdust was as fragrant, as sound, and as pink as our own. An oak is no respecter of persons.

The reign of the bootlegger ended sometime during the dust-bowl drouths of 1936, 1934, 1933, and 1930. Oak smoke from his still and peat from burning marshlands must have clouded the sun in those years, and alphabetical conservation was abroad in the land, but the sawdust shows no change.

Rest! cries the chief sawyer, and we pause for breath.

* * *

Now our saw bites into the 1920's, the Babbittian decade when everything grew bigger and better in heedlessness and arrogance—until 1929, when stock markets crumpled. If the oak heard them fall, its wood gives no sign. Nor did it heed the Legislature's several protestations of love for trees: a National Forest and a forest-crop law in 1927, a great refuge on the Upper Mississippi bottomlands in 1924, and a new forest policy in 1921. Neither did it notice the demise of the state's last marten in 1925, nor the arrival of its first starling in 1923.

In March 1922, the 'Big Sleet' tore the neighboring elms limb from limb, but there is no sign of damage to our tree. What is a ton of ice, more or less, to a good oak?

Rest! cries the chief sawyer, and we pause for breath.

*   *   *

Now the saw bites into 1910–20, the decade of the drainage dream, when steam shovels sucked dry the marshes of central Wisconsin to make farms, and made ash-heaps instead. Our marsh escaped, not because of any caution or forbearance among engineers, but because the river floods it each April, and did so with a vengeance—perhaps a defensive vengeance—in the years 1913–16. The oak laid on wood just the same, even in 1915, when the Supreme Court abolished the state forests and Governor Phillip pontificated that 'state forestry is not a good business proposition.' (It did not occur to the Governor that there might be more than one definition of what is good, and even of what is business. It did not occur to him that while the courts were writing one definition of goodness in the law books, fires were writing quite another one on the face of the land. Perhaps, to be a governor, one must be free from doubt on such matters.)

While forestry receded during this decade, game conservation advanced. In 1916 pheasants became successfully established in Waukesha County; in 1915 a federal law prohibited spring shooting; in 1913 a state game farm was started; in 1912 a 'buck law' protected female deer; in 1911 an epidemic of refuges spread over the state. 'Refuge' became a holy word, but the oak took no heed.

Rest! cries the chief sawyer, and we pause for breath.

*   *   *

Now we cut 1910, when a great university president published a book on conservation, a great sawfly epidemic killed millions of tamaracks, a great drouth burned the pineries, and a great dredge drained Horicon Marsh.

We cut 1909, when smelt were first planted in the Greak Lakes, and when a wet summer induced the Legislature to cut the forest-fire appropriations.

We cut 1908, a dry year when the forests burned fiercely, and Wisconsin parted with its last cougar.

We cut 1907, when a wandering lynx, looking in the wrong direction for the promised land, ended his career among the farms of Dane County.

We cut 1906, when the first state forester took office, and fires burned 17,000 acres in these sand counties; we cut 1905 when a great flight of goshawks came out of the North and ate up the local grouse (they no doubt perched in this tree to eat some of mine). We cut 1902–3, a winter of bitter cold; 1901, which brought the most intense drouth of record (rainfall only 17 inches); 1900, a centennial year of hope, of prayer, and the usual annual ring of oak.

Rest! cries the chief sawyer, and we pause for breath.

*   *   *

Now our saw bites into the 1890's, called gay by those whose eyes turn cityward rather than land-ward. We cut 1899, when the last passenger pigeon collided with a charge of shot near Babcock, two counties to the north; we cut 1898 when a dry fall, followed by a snowless winter, froze the soil seven feet deep and killed the apple trees; 1897, another drouth year, when another forestry commission came into being; 1896, when 25,000 prairie chickens were shipped to market from the village of Spooner alone; 1895, another year of fires; 1894, another drouth year; and 1893, the year of 'The Bluebird Storm,' when a March blizzard reduced the migrating bluebirds to near-zero. (The first bluebirds always alighted in this oak, but in the middle 'nineties it must have gone without.) We cut 1892, another year of fires; 1891, a low in the grouse cycle; and 1890, the year of the Babcock Milk Tester, which enabled Governor Heil to boast, half a century later, that Wisconsin is Amer-ica's Dairyland. The motor licenses which now parade that boast were then not foreseen, even by Professor Babcock.

It was likewise in 1890 that the largest pine rafts in history slipped down the Wisconsin River in full view of my oak, to build an empire of red barns for the cows of the prairie states. Thus it is that good pine now stands between the cow and the blizzard, just as good oak stands between the blizzard and me.

Rest! cries the chief sawyer, and we pause for breath.

*   *   *

Now our saw bites into the 1880's; into 1889, a drouth year in which Arbor Day was first proclaimed; into 1887, when Wisconsin appointed its first game wardens; into 1886, when the College of Agriculture held its first short course for farmers; into 1885, preceded by a winter 'of unprecedented length and severity'; into 1883, when Dean W. H. Henry reported that the spring flowers at Madison bloomed 13 days later than average; into 1882, the year Lake Mendota opened a month late following the historic 'Big Snow' and bitter cold of 1881–2.

It was likewise in 1881 that the Wisconsin Agricultural Society debated the question, 'How do you account for the second growth of black oak timber that has sprung up all over the country in the last thirty years?' My oak was one of these. One debater claimed spontaneous generation, another claimed regurgitation of acorns by southbound pigeons.

Rest! cries the chief sawyer, and we pause for breath.

*   *   *

Now our saw bites the 1870's, the decade of Wisconsin's carousal in wheat. Monday morning came in 1879, when chinch bugs, grubs, rust, and soil exhaustion finally convinced Wisconsin farmers that they could not compete with the virgin prairies further west in the game of wheating land to death. I suspect that this farm played its share in the game, and that the sand blow just north of my oak had its origin in over-wheating.

This same year of 1879 saw the first planting of carp in Wisconsin, and also the first arrival of quack-grass as a stowaway from Europe. On 27 October 1879, six migrating prairie chickens perched on the rooftree of the German Methodist Church in Madison, and took a look at the growing city. On 8 November the markets at Madison were reported to be glutted with ducks at 10 cents each.

In 1878 a deer hunter from Sauk Rapids remarked prophetically, 'The hunters promise to outnumber the deer.'

On 10 September 1877, two brothers, shooting Muskego Lake, bagged 210 blue-winged teal in one day.

In 1876 came the wettest year of record; the rainfall piled up 50 inches. Prairie chickens declined, perhaps owing to hard rains.

In 1875 four hunters killed 153 prairie chickens at York Prairie, one county to the eastward. In the same year the U.S. Fish Commission planted Atlantic salmon in Devil's Lake, 10 miles south of my oak.

In 1874 the first factory-made barbed wire was stapled to oak trees; I hope no such artifacts are buried in the oak now under saw!

In 1873 one Chicago firm received and marketed 25,000 prairie chickens. The Chicago trade collectively bought 600,000 at $3.25 per dozen.

In 1872 the last wild Wisconsin turkey was killed, two counties to the southwest.

It is appropriate that the decade ending the pioneer carousal in wheat should likewise have ended the pioneer carousal in pigeon blood. In 1871, within a 50-mile triangle spreading northwestward from my oak, 136 million pigeons are estimated to have nested, and some may have nested in it, for it was then a thrifty sapling 20 feet tall. Pigeon hunters by scores plied their trade with net and gun, club and salt lick, and trainloads of prospective pigeon pie moved southward and eastward toward the cities. It was the last big nesting in Wisconsin, and nearly the last in any state.

This same year 1871 brought other evidence of the march of empire: the Peshtigo Fire, which cleared a couple of counties of trees and soil, and the Chicago Fire, said to have started from the protesting kick of a cow.

In 1870 the meadow mice had already staged their march of empire; they ate up the young orchards of the young state, and then died. They did not eat my oak, whose bark was already too tough and thick for mice.

It was likewise in 1870 that a market gunner boasted in the *American Sportsman* of killing 6000 ducks in one season near Chicago.

Rest! cries the chief sawyer, and we pause for breath.

*   *   *

Our saw now cuts the 1860's, when thousands died to settle the question: Is the man-man community lightly to be dismembered? They settled it, but they did not see, nor do we yet see, that the same question applies to the man-land community.

This decade was not without its gropings toward the larger issue. In 1867 Increase A. Lapham induced the State Horticultural Society to offer prizes for forest plantations. In 1866 the last native Wisconsin elk was killed. The saw now severs 1865, the pith-year of our oak. In that year John Muir offered to buy from his brother, who then owned the home farm thirty miles east of my oak, a sanctuary for the wild-flowers that had gladdened his youth. His brother declined to part with the land, but he could not sup-press the idea: 1865 still stands in Wisconsin history as the birthyear of mercy for things natural, wild, and free.

We have cut the core. Our saw now reverses its orientation in history; we cut backward across the years, and outward toward the far side of the stump. At last there is a tremor in the great trunk; the saw-kerf suddenly widens; the saw is quickly pulled as the sawyers spring backward to safety; all hands cry 'Timber!'; my oak leans, groans, and crashes with earth-shaking thunder, to lie prostrate across the emigrant road that gave it birth.

*　　　　*　　　　*

Now comes the job of making wood. The maul rings on steel wedges as the sections of trunk are up-ended one by one, only to fall apart in fragrant slabs to be corded by the roadside.

There is an allegory for historians in the diverse functions of saw, wedge, and axe.

The saw works only across the years, which it must deal with one by one, in sequence. From each year the raker teeth pull little chips of fact, which accumulate in little piles, called sawdust by woodsmen and archives by historians; both judge the character of what lies within by the character of the samples thus made visible without. It is not until the transect is completed that the tree falls, and the stump yields a collective view of a century. By its fall the tree attests the unity of the hodge-podge called history.

The wedge, on the other hand, works only in radial splits; such a split yields a collective view of all the years at once, or no view at all, depending on the skill with which the plane of the split is chosen. (If in doubt, let the section season for a year until a crack develops. Many a hastily driven wedge lies rusting in the woods, embedded in unsplittable cross-grain.)

The axe functions only at an angle diagonal to the years, and this only for the peripheral rings of the recent past. Its special function is to lop limbs, for which both saw and wedge are useless.

The three tools are requisite to good oak, and to good history.

*　　　　　　*　　　　　　*

These things I ponder as the kettle sings, and the good oak burns to red coals on white ashes. Those ashes, come spring, I will return to the orchard at the foot of the sandhill. They will come back to me again, perhaps as red apples, or perhaps as a spirit of enterprise in some fat October squirrel, who, for reasons unknown to himself, is bent on planting acorns.

March

The Geese Return

ONE SWALLOW does not make a summer, but one skein of geese, cleaving the murk of a March thaw, is the spring.

A cardinal, whistling spring to a thaw but later finding himself mistaken, can retrieve his error by resuming his winter silence. A chipmunk, emerging for a sunbath but finding a blizzard, has only to go back to bed. But a migrating goose, staking two hundred miles of black night on the chance of finding a hole in the lake, has no easy chance for retreat. His arrival carries the conviction of a prophet who has burned his bridges.

A March morning is only as drab as he who walks in it without a glance skyward, ear cocked for geese. I once knew an educated lady, banded by Phi Beta Kappa, who told me that she had never heard or seen the geese that twice a year proclaim the revolving seasons to her well-insulated roof. Is education possibly a process of trading awareness for things of lesser worth? The goose who trades his is soon a pile of feathers.

The geese that proclaim the seasons to our farm are aware of many things, including the Wisconsin statutes. The southbound November flocks pass over us high and haughty, with scarcely a honk of recognition for their favorite sandbars and sloughs. 'As a crow flies' is crooked compared with their undeviating aim at the nearest big lake twenty miles to the south, where they loaf by day on broad waters and filch corn by night from the freshly cut stubbles. November geese are aware that every marsh and pond bristles from dawn till dark with hopeful guns.

March geese are a different story. Although they have been shot at most of the winter, as attested by their buckshot-battered pinions, they know that the spring truce is now in effect. They wind the oxbows of the river, cutting low over the now gunless points and islands, and gabbling to each sandbar as to a long-lost friend. They weave low over the marshes and meadows, greeting each newly melted puddle and pool. Finally, after a few *pro-forma* circlings of our marsh, they set wing and glide silently to the pond, black landing-gear lowered and rumps white against the far hill. Once touching water, our newly arrived guests set up a honking and splashing that shakes the last thought of winter out of the brittle cattails. Our geese are home again!

It is at this moment of each year that I wish I were a muskrat, eye-deep in the marsh.

Once the first geese are in, they honk a clamorous invitation to each migrating flock, and in a few days the marsh is full of them. On our farm we measure the amplitude of our spring by two yardsticks: the number of pines planted, and the number of geese that stop. Our record is 642 geese counted in on 11 April 1946.

As in fall, our spring geese makes daily trips to corn, but these are no surreptitious sneakings-out by night; the flocks move noisily to and from corn stubbles through the day. Each departure is preceded by loud gustatory debate, and each return by an even louder one. The returning flocks, once thoroughly at home, omit their *pro-forma* circlings of the marsh. They tumble out of the sky like maple leaves, side-slipping right and left to lose altitude, feet spraddled toward the shouts of welcome below. I suppose the ensuing gabble deals with the merits of the day's dinner. They are now eating the waste corn that the snow blanket has protected over winter from corn-seeking crows, cottontails, meadow mice, and pheasants.

It is a conspicuous fact that the corn stubbles selected by geese for feeding are usually those occupying former prairies. No man knows whether this bias for prairie corn reflects some superior nutritional value, or some ancestral tradition transmitted from generation to generation since the prairie days. Perhaps it reflects the simpler fact that prairie cornfields tend to be large. If I could understand the thunderous debates that precede and follow these daily excursions to corn, I might soon learn the reason for the prairie-bias. But I cannot, and I am well content that it should remain a mystery. What a dull world if we knew all about geese!

In thus watching the daily routine of a spring goose convention, one notices the prevalence of singles—lone geese that do much flying about and much talking. One is apt to impute a disconsolate tone to their honkings, and to jump to the conclusion that they are broken-hearted widowers, or mothers hunting lost children. The seasoned ornithologist knows, however, that such subjective interpretation of bird behavior is risky. I long tried to keep an open mind on the question.

After my students and I had counted for half a dozen years the number of geese comprising a flock, some unexpected light was cast on the meaning of lone geese. It was found by mathematical analysis that flocks of six or multiples of six were far more frequent than chance alone would dictate. In other words, goose flocks are families, or aggregations of families, and lone geese in spring are probably just what our fond imaginings had first suggested. They are bereaved survivors of the winter's shooting, searching in vain for their kin. Now I am free to grieve with and for the lone honkers.

It is not often that cold-potato mathematics thus confirms the sentimental promptings of the bird-lover.

On April nights when it has become warm enough to sit outdoors, we love to listen to the proceedings of the convention in the marsh. There are long periods of silence when one hears only the winnowing of snipe, the hoot of a distant owl, or the nasal clucking of some amorous coot. Then, of a sudden, a strident honk resounds, and in an instant pandemonium echoes. There is a beating of pinions on water, a rushing of dark prows propelled by churning paddles, and a general shouting by the onlookers of a vehement controversy. Finally some deep honker has his last word, and the noise subsides to that half-audible small-talk that seldom ceases among geese. Once again, I would I were a muskrat!

By the time the pasques are in full bloom our goose-convention dwindles, and before May our marsh is once again a mere grassy wetness, enlivened only by redwings and rails.

*　　　　　*　　　　　*

It is an irony of history that the great powers should have discovered the unity of nations at Cairo in 1943. The geese of the world have had that notion for a longer time, and each March they stake their lives on its essential truth.

In the beginning there was only the unity of the Ice Sheet. Then followed the unity of the March thaw, and the northward hegira of the international geese. Every March since the Pleistocene, the geese have honked unity from China Sea to Siberian Steppe, from Euphrates to Volga, from Nine to Murmansk, from Lincolnshire to Spitsbergen. Every March since the Pleistocene, the geese have honked unity from

Currituck to Labrador, Matamuskeet to Ungava, Horseshoe Lake to Hudson's Bay, Avery Island to Baffin Land, Panhandle to Mackenzie, Sacramento to Yukon.

By this international commerce of geese, the waste corn of Illinois is carried through the clouds of the Arctic tundras, there to combine with the waste sunlight of a nightless June to grow goslings for all the lands between. And in this annual barter of food for light, and winter warmth for summer solitude, the whole continent receives as net profit a wild poem dropped from the murky skies upon the muds of March.

April

Come High Water

THE SAME logic that causes big rivers always to flow past big cities causes cheap farms sometimes to be marooned by spring floods. Ours is a cheap farm, and sometimes when we visit it in April we get marooned.

Not intentionally, of course, but one can, to a degree, guess from weather reports when the snows up north will melt, and one can estimate how many days it takes for the flood to run the gauntlet of upriver cities. Thus, come Sunday evening, one must go back to town and work, but one can't. How sweetly the spreading waters murmur condolence for the wreckage they have inflicted on Monday morning dates! How deep and chesty the honkings of the geese as they cruise over cornfield after cornfield, each in process of becoming a lake. Every hundred yards some new goose flails the air as he struggles to lead the echelon in its morning survey of this new and watery world.

The enthusiasm of geese for high water is a subtle thing, and might be overlooked by those unfamiliar with goose-gossip, but the enthusiasm of carp is obvious and unmistakable. No sooner has the rising flood wetted the grass roots than here they come, rooting and wallowing with the prodigious zest of pigs turned out to pasture, flashing red tails and yellow bellies, cruising the wagon tracks and cow-paths, and shaking the reeds and bushes in their haste to explore what to them is an expanding universe.

Unlike the geese and the carp, the terrestrial birds and mammals accept high water with philosophical detachment. A cardinal atop a river birch whistles loudly his claim to a territory that, but for the trees, cannot be seen to exist. A ruffed grouse drums from the flooded woods; he must be perched on the high end of his highest drumming log. Meadow-mice paddle ridgeward with the calm assurance of miniature muskrats. From the orchard bounds a deer, evicted from his usual daytime bed in the willow thickets. Everywhere are rabbits, calmly accepting quarters on our hill, which serves, in Noah's absence, for an ark.

The spring flood brings us more than high adventure; it brings likewise an unpredictable miscellany of floatable objects pilfered from upriver farms. An old board stranded on our meadow has, to us, twice the value of the same piece new from the lumberyard. Each old board has its own individual history, always unknown, but always to some degree guessable from the kind of wood, its dimensions, its nails, screws, or paint, its finish or the lack of it, its wear or decay. One can even guess, from the abrasion of its edges and ends on sandbars, how many floods have carried it in years past.

Our lumber pile, recruited entirely from the river, is thus not only a collection of personalities, but an anthology of human strivings in upriver farms and forests. The autobiography of an old board is a kind of literature not yet taught on campuses, but any riverbank farm is a library where he who hammers or saws may read at will. Come high water, there is always an accession of new books.

*   *   *

There are degrees and kinds of solitude. An island in a lake has one kind; but lakes have boats, and there is always the chance that one might land to pay you a visit. A peak in the clouds has another kind; but most peaks have trails, and trails have tourists. I know of no solitude so secure as one guarded by a spring flood; nor do the geese, who have seen more kinds and degrees of aloneness than I have.

So we sit on our hill beside a new-blown pasque, and watch the geese go by. I see our road dipping gently into the waters, and I conclude (with inner glee but exterior detachment) that the question of traffic, in or out, is for this day at least, debatable only among carp.

Draba

Within a few weeks now Draba, the smallest flower
that blows, will sprinkle every sandy place with small
blooms.

He who hopes for spring with upturned eye
never sees so small a thing as Draba. He who despairs
of spring with downcast eye steps on it, unknowing.
He who searches for spring with his knees in the mud
finds it, in abundance.

Draba asks, and gets, but scant allowance of warmth
and comfort; it subsists on the leavings of unwanted
time and space. Botany books give it two or three
lines, but never a plate or portrait. Sand too poor
and sun too weak for bigger, better blooms are good
enough for Draba. After all it is no spring flower, but
only a postscript to a hope.

Draba plucks no heartstrings. Its perfume, if there
is any, is lost in the gusty winds. Its color is plain
white. Its leaves wear a sensible woolly coat. Nothing
eats it; it is too small. No poets sing of it. Some botanist once gave it a Latin name, and then forgot it.
Altogether it is of no importance—just a small creature that does a small job quickly and well.

Bur Oak

When school children vote on a state bird, flower or
tree, they are not making a decision; they are merely
ratifying history. Thus history made bur oak the
characteristic tree of southern Wisconsin when the
prairie grasses first gained possession of the region.

Bur oak is the only tree that can stand up to a prairie fire and live.

Have you ever wondered why a thick crust of corky bark covers the whole tree, even to the smallest twigs? This cork is armor. Bur oaks were the shock troops sent by the invading forest to storm the prairie; fire is what they had to fight. Each April, before the new grasses had covered the prairie with unburnable greenery, fires ran at will over the land, sparing only such old oaks as had grown bark too thick to scorch. Most of these groves of scattered veterans, known to the pioneers as 'oak openings,' consisted of bur oaks.

Engineers did not discover insulation; they copied it from these old soldiers of the prairie war. Botanists can read the story of that war for twenty thousand years. The record consists partly of pollen grains embedded in peats, partly of relic plants interned in the rear of the battle, and there forgotten. The record shows that the forest front at times retreated almost to Lake Superior; at times it advanced far to the south. At one period it advanced so far southward that spruce and other 'rear guard' species grew to and beyond the southern border of Wisconsin; spruce pollen appears at a certain level in all peat bogs of the region. But the average battle line between prairie and forest was about where it is now, and the net outcome of the battle was a draw.

One reason for this was that there were allies that threw their support first to one side, then to the other. Thus rabbits and mice mowed down the prairie herbs in summer, and in winter girdled any oak seedlings that survived the fires. Squirrels planted acorns in fall, and ate them all the rest of the year.

June beetles undermined the prairie sod in their grub stage, but defoliated the oaks in their adult stage. But for this geeing and hawing of allies, and hence of the victory, we should not have today that rich mosaic of prairie and forest soils which looks so decorative on a map.

Jonathan Carver has left us a vivid word picture of the prairie border in pre-settlement days. On 10 October 1763, he visited Blue Mounds, a group of high hills (now wooded) near the southwestern corner of Dane County. He says:

I ascended one of the highest of these, and had an extensive view of the country. For many miles nothing was to be seen but lesser mountains, which appeared at a distance like haycocks, they being free from trees. Only a few groves of hickory, and stunted oaks, covered some of the vallies.

In the 1840's a new animal, the settler, intervened in the prairie battle. He didn't mean to, he just plowed enough fields to deprive the prairie of its immemorial ally: fire. Seedling oaks forthwith romped over the grasslands in legions, and what had been the prairie region became a region of woodlot farms. If you doubt this story, go count the rings on any set of stumps on any 'ridge' woodlot in southwest Wisconsin. All the trees except the oldest veterans date back to the 1850's and the 1860's, and this was when fires ceased on the prairie.

John Muir grew up in Marquette County during this period when new woods overrode the old prairies and engulfed the oak openings in thickets of saplings. In his *Boyhood and Youth* he recalls that:

The uniformly rich soil of the Illinois and Wisconsin prairies produced so close and tall a growth of grasses for fires that no tree could live on it. Had there been no fires, these fine prairies, so marked a feature of the country, would have been covered by the heaviest forest. As soon as the oak openings were settled, and the farmers had prevented running grass-fires, the grubs [roots] grew up into trees and formed tall-thickets so dense that it was difficult to walk through them, and every trace of the sunny [oak] 'openings' vanished.

Thus, he who owns a veteran bur oak owns more than a tree. He owns a historical library, and a reserved seat in the theater of evolution. To the discerning eye, his farm is labeled with the badge and symbol of the prairie war.

Sky Dance

I owned my farm for two years before learning that the sky dance is to be seen over my woods every evening in April and May. Since we discovered it, my family and I have been reluctant to miss even a single performance.

The show begins on the first warm evening in April at exactly 6:50 p.m. The curtain goes up one minute later each day until 1 June, when the time is 7:50. This sliding scale is dictated by vanity, the dancer demanding a romantic light intensity of exactly 0.05 foot-candles. Do not be late, and sit quietly, lest he fly away in a huff.

The stage props, like the opening hour, reflect the temperamental demands of the performer. The stage must be an open amphitheater in woods or brush, and in its center there must be a mossy spot, a streak of sterile sand, a bare outcrop of rock, or a bare roadway. Why the male woodcock should be such a stickler for a bare dance floor puzzled me at first, but I now think it is a matter of legs. The woodcock's legs are short, and his struttings cannot be executed to advantage in dense grass or weeds, nor could his lady see them there. I have more woodcocks than most farmers because I have more mossy sand, too poor to support grass.

Knowing the place and the hour, you seat yourself under a bush to the east of the dance floor and wait, watching against the sunset for the woodcock's arrival. He flies in low from some neighboring thicket, alights on the bare moss, and at once begins the overture: a series of queer throaty *peents* spaced about two seconds apart, and sounding much like the summer call of the nighthawk.

Suddenly the peenting ceases and the bird flutters skyward in a series of wide spirals, emitting a musical twitter. Up and up he goes, the spirals steeper and smaller, the twittering louder and louder, until the performer is only a speck in the sky. Then, without warning, he tumbles like a crippled plane, giving voice in a soft liquid warble that a March bluebird might envy. At a few feet from the ground he levels off and returns to his peenting ground, usually to the exact spot where the performance began, and there resumes his peenting.

It is soon too dark to see the bird on the ground, but you can see his flights against the sky for an hour, which is the usual duration of the show. On moonlight nights, however, it may continue, at intervals, as long as the moon continues to shine.

At daybreak the whole show is repeated. In early April the final curtain falls at 5:15 a.m.; the time advances two minutes a day until June, when the performance closes for the year at 3:15. Why the disparity in sliding scale? Alas, I fear that even romance tires, for it takes only a fifth as much light to stop the sky dance at dawn as suffices to start it at sunset.

*   *   *

It is fortunate, perhaps, that no matter how intently one studies the hundred little dramas of the woods and meadows, one can never learn all of the salient facts about any one of them. What I do not yet know about the sky dance is: where is the lady, and just what part, if any, does she play? I often see two woodcocks on a peenting ground, and the two sometimes fly together, but they never peent together. Is the second bird the hen, or a rival male?

Another unknown: is the twitter vocal, or is it mechanical? My friend, Bill Feeney, once clapped a net over a peenting bird and removed his outer primary wing feathers; thereafter the bird peented and warbled, but twittered no more. But one such experiment is hardly conclusive.

Another unknown: up to what stage of nesting does the male continue the sky dance? My daughter once saw a bird peenting within twenty yards of a nest containing hatched eggshells, but was this *his* lady's

nest? Or is this secretive fellow possibly bigamous
without our ever having found it out? These, and
many other questions, remain mysteries of the deep-
ening dusk.

The drama of the sky dance is enacted nightly on
hundreds of farms, the owners of which sigh for entertainment, but harbor the illusion that it is to
be sought in theaters. They live on the land, but not
by the land.

The woodcock is a living refutation of the theory
that the utility of a game bird is to serve as a target,
or to pose gracefully on a slice of toast. No one would
rather hunt woodcock in October than I, but since
learning of the sky dance I find myself calling one or
two birds enough. I must be sure that, come April,
there be no dearth of dancers in the sunset sky.

May

Back from the Argentine

WHEN DANDELIONS have set the mark of May on Wisconsin pastures, it is time to listen for the final proof of spring. Sit down on a tussock, cock your ears at the sky, dial out the bedlam of meadowlarks and redwings, and soon you may hear it: the flight-song of the upland plover, just now back from the Argentine.

If your eyes are strong, you may search the sky and see him, wings aquiver, circling among the woolly clouds. If your eyes are weak, don't try it; just watch the fence posts. Soon a flash of silver will tell you on which post the plover has alighted and folded his long wings. Whoever invented the word 'grace' must have seen the wing-folding of the plover.

There he sits; his whole being says it's your next move to absent yourself from his domain. The county records may allege that you own this pasture, but the plover airily rules out such trivial legalities. He has just flown 4000 miles to reassert the title he got from the Indians, and until the young plovers are a-wing, this pasture is his, and none may trespass without his protest.

Somewhere near by, the hen plover is brooding

the four large pointed eggs which will shortly hatch four precocial chicks. From the moment their down is dry, they scamper through the grass like mice on stilts, quite able to elude your clumsy efforts to catch them. At thirty days the chicks are full grown; no other fowl develops with equal speed. By August they have graduated from flying school, and on cool August nights you can hear their whistled signals as they set wing for the pampas, to prove again the age-old unity of the Americas. Hemisphere solidarity is new among statesmen, but not among the feathered navies of the sky.

The upland plover fits easily into the agricultural countryside. He follows the black-and-white buffalo, which now pasture his prairies, and finds them an acceptable substitute for brown ones. He nests in hay-fields as well as pastures, but, unlike the clumsy pheasant, does not get caught in hay mowers. Well before the hay is ready to cut, the young plovers are a-wing and away. In farm country, the plover has only two real enemies: the gully and the drainage ditch. Perhaps we shall one day find that these are our enemies, too.

There was a time in the early 1900's when Wisconsin farms nearly lost their immemorial timepiece, when May pastures greened in silence, and August nights brought no whistled reminder of impending fall. Universal gunpowder, plus the lure of plover-on-toast for post-Victorian banquets, had taken too great a toll. The belated protection of the federal migratory bird laws came just in time.

June

The Alder Fork—A Fishing Idyl

WE FOUND the main stream so low that the teeter-snipe pattered about in what last year were trout riffles, and so warm that we could duck in its deepest pool without a shout. Even after our cooling swim, waders felt like hot tar paper in the sun.

The evening's fishing proved as disappointing as its auguries. We asked that stream for trout, and it gave us a chub. That night we sat under a mosquito smudge and debated the morrow's plan. Two hundred miles of hot, dusty road we had come, to feel again the impetuous tug of a disillusioned brook or rainbow. There were no trout.

But this, we now remembered, was a stream of parts. High up near the headwaters we had once seen a fork, narrow, deep, and fed by cold springs that gurgled out under its close-hemmed walls of alder. What would a self-respecting trout do in such weather? Just what we did: go up.

In the fresh of the morning, when a hundred whitethroats had forgotten it would ever again be anything but sweet and cool, I climbed down the dewy bank and stepped into the Alder Fork. A trout was rising just upstream. I paid out some line—

wishing it would always stay thus soft and dry—and, measuring the distance with a false cast or two, laid down a spent gnat exactly a foot above his last swirl. Forgotten now were the hot miles, the mosquitoes, the ignominious chub. He took it with one great gulp, and shortly I could hear him kicking in the bed of wet alder leaves at the bottom of the creel.

Another, albeit larger, fish had meanwhile risen in the next pool, which lay at the very 'head of navigation,' for at its upper end the alders closed in solid phalanx. One bush, with its brown stem laved in the middle current, shook with a perpetual silent laughter, as if to mock at any fly that gods or men might cast one inch beyond its outermost leaf.

*　　　　　*　　　　　*

For the duration of a cigarette I sit on a rock midstream—and watch my trout rise under his guardian bush, while my rod and line hang drying on the alders of the sunny bank. Then—for prudence' sake—a little longer. That pool is too smooth up there. A breeze is stirring and may shortly ruffle it for an instant, and thus make more deadly that perfect cast I shall shortly lay upon its bosom.

It will come—a puff strong enough to shake a brown miller off the laughing alder, and cast it upon the pool.

Ready now! Coil up the dry line and stand midstream, rod in instant readiness. It's coming—a little premonitory shiver in that aspen on the hill lets me get out half a cast, and swish it gently back and forth, ready for the main puff to hit the pool. No more than half a line, mind you! The sun is high now, and any flicking shadow overhead would forewarn my hunker of his impending fate. Now! The last three yards shoot out, the fly falls gracefully at the feet of the laughing alder—he has it! I set hard to hold him out of the jungle beyond. He rushes downstream. In a few minutes he, too, is kicking in the creel.

I sit in happy meditation on my rock, pondering, while my line dries again, upon the ways of trout and men. How like fish we are: ready, nay eager, to seize upon whatever new thing some wind of circumstance shakes down upon the river of time! And how we rue our haste, finding the gilded morsel to contain a hook. Even so, I think there is some virtue in eagerness, whether its object prove true or false. How utterly dull would be a wholly prudent man, or trout, or world! Did I say a while ago that I waited 'for prudence' sake'? That was not so. The only prudence in fishermen is that designed to set the stage for taking yet another, and perhaps a longer, chance.

Time to be at it now—they will soon stop rising. I wade waist deep to head of navigation, poke my head insolently into the shaking alder, and look within. Jungle is right! A coal-black hole above, so canopied in greenness you could not wave a fern, much less a rod, above its rushing depths. And there, almost rubbing his ribs against the dark bank, a great trout rolls lazily over as he sucks down a passing bug.

Not a chance to stalk him, even with the lowly worm. But twenty yards above I see bright sunshine on the water—another opening. Fish a dry fly downstream? It cannot, but it must, be done.

I retreat and climb the bank. Neck deep in jewelweed and nettles, I detour through the alder thicket to the opening above. With cat-like care not to roil his majesty's bath, I step in, and stand stock-still for five minutes to let things calm down. The while, I strip out, oil, dry, and coil upon my left hand thirty feet of line. I am that far above the portal to the jungle.

Now for the long chance! I blow upon my fly to give it one last fluff, lay it on the stream at my feet, and quickly pay out coil after coil. Then, just as the line straightens out and the fly is sucked into the jungle, I walk quickly downstream, straining my eyes into the dark vault to follow its fortunes. A fleeting glimpse or two as it passes a speck of sunlight shows it still rides clear. It rounds the bend. In no time— long before the roil of my walking has betrayed the ruse—it reaches the black pool. I hear, rather than see, the rush of the great fish; I set hard, and the battle is on.

No prudent man would risk a dollar's worth of fly and leader pulling a trout upstream through the giant tooth-brush of alder stems comprising the bend of that creek. But, as I said, no prudent man is a fisherman. By and by, with much cautious unraveling, I got him up into open water, and finally aboard the creel.

I shall now confess to you that none of those three trout had to be beheaded, or folded double, to fit their casket. What was big was not the trout, but the chance. What was full was not my creel, but my memory. Like the white-throats, I had forgotten it would ever again be aught but morning on the Fork.

July

Great Possessions

ONE HUNDRED and twenty acres, according to the County Clerk, is the extent of my worldly domain. But the County Clerk is a sleepy fellow, who never looks at his record books before nine o'clock. What they would show at daybreak is the question here at issue.

Books or no books, it is a fact, patent both to my dog and myself, that at daybreak I am the sole owner of all the acres I can walk over. It is not only boundaries that disappear, but also the thought of being bounded. Expanses unknown to deed or map are known to every dawn, and solitude, supposed no longer to exist in my county, extends on every hand as far as the dew can reach.

Like other great landowners, I have tenants. They are negligent about rents, but very punctilious about tenures. Indeed at every daybreak from April to July they proclaim their boundaries to each other, and so acknowledge, at least by inference, their fiefdom to me.

This daily ceremony, contrary to what you might suppose, begins with the utmost decorum. Who originally laid down its protocols I do not know. At 3:30 a.m., with such dignity as I can muster of a

July morning, I step from my cabin door, bearing in either hand my emblems of sovereignty, a coffee pot and notebook. I seat myself on a bench, facing the white wake of the morning star. I set the pot beside me. I extract a cup from my shirt front, hoping none will notice its informal mode of transport. I get out my watch, pour coffee, and lay notebook on knee. This is the cue for the proclamations to begin.

At 3:35 the nearest field sparrow avows, in a clear tenor chant, that he holds the jackpine copse north to the riverbank, and south to the old wagon track. One by one all the other field sparrows within earshot recite their respective holdings. There are no disputes, at least at this hour, so I just listen, hoping inwardly that their womenfolk acquiesce in this happy accord over the *status quo ante*.

Before the field sparrows have quite gone the rounds, the robin in the big elm warbles loudly his claim to the crotch where the icestorm tore off a limb, and all appurtenances pertaining thereto (meaning, in his case, all the angleworms in the not-very-spacious subjacent lawn).

The robin's insistent caroling awakens the oriole, who now tells the world of orioles that the pendant branch of the elm belongs to him, together with all fiber-bearing milkweed stalks near by, all loose strings in the garden, and the exclusive right to flash like a burst of fire from one of these to another.

My watch says 3:50. The indigo bunting on the hill asserts title to the dead oak limb left by the 1936 drought, and to divers near-by bugs and bushes. He does not claim, but I think he implies, the right to out-blue all bluebirds, and all spiderworts that have turned their faces to the dawn.

Next the wren—the one who discovered the knot-hole in the eave of the cabin—explodes into song. Half a dozen other wrens give voice, and now all is bedlam. Grosbeaks, thrashers, yellow warblers, blue-birds, vireos, towhees, cardinals—all are at it. My solemn list of performers, in their order and time of first song, hesitates, wavers, ceases, for my ear can no longer filter out priorities. Besides, the pot is empty and the sun is about to rise. I must inspect my domain before my title runs out.

We sally forth, the dog and I, at random. He has paid scant respect to all these vocal goings-on, for to

him the evidence of tenantry is not song, but scent. Any illiterate bundle of feathers, he says, can make a noise in a tree. Now he is going to translate for me the olfactory poems that who-knows-what silent crea-tures have written in the summer night. At the end of each poem sits the author—if we can find him. What we actually find is beyond predicting: a rabbit, suddenly yearning to be elsewhere; a woodcock, fluttering his disclaimer; a cock pheasant, indignant over wetting his feathers in the grass.

Once in a while we turn up a coon or mink, returning late from the night's foray. Sometimes we rout a heron from his unfinished fishing, or surprise a mother wood duck with her convoy of ducklings, headed full-steam for the shelter of the pickerelweeds. Sometimes we see deer sauntering back to the thickets, replete with alfalfa blooms, veronica, and wild lettuce. More often we see only the interweaving darkened lines that lazy hoofs have traced on the silken fabric of the dew.

I can feel the sun now. The bird-chorus has run out of breath. The far clank of cowbells bespeaks a herd ambling to pasture. A tractor roars warning that my neighbor is astir. The world has shrunk to those mean dimensions known to county clerks. We turn toward home, and breakfast.

Prairie Birthday

During every week from April to September there are, on the average, ten wild plants coming into first bloom. In June as many as a dozen species may burst their buds on a single day. No man can heed all of these anniversaries; no man can ignore all of them. He who steps unseeing on May dandelions may be hauled up short by August ragweed pollen; he who ignores the ruddy haze of April elms may skid his car on the fallen corollas of June catalpas. Tell me of what plant-birthday a man takes notice, and I shall tell you a good deal about his vocation, his hobbies, his hay fever, and the general level of his ecological education.

*   *   *

Every July I watch eagerly a certain country grave-yard that I pass in driving to and from my farm. It is time for a prairie birthday, and in one corner of this graveyard lives a surviving celebrant of that once important event.

It is an ordinary graveyard, bordered by the usual spruces, and studded with the usual pink granite or white marble headstones, each with the usual Sunday

bouquet of red or pink geraniums. It is extraordinary only in being triangular instead of square, and in harboring, within the sharp angle of its fence, a pin-point remnant of the native prairie on which the graveyard was established in the 1840's. Heretofore unreachable by scythe or mower, this yard-square relic of original Wisconsin gives birth, each July, to a man-high stalk of compass plant or cutleaf Silphium, spangled with saucer-sized yellow blooms resembling sunflowers. It is the sole remnant of this plant along this highway, and perhaps the sole remnant in the western half of our county. What a thousand acres of Silphiums looked like when they tickled the bellies of the buffalo is a question never again to be answered, and perhaps not even asked.

This year I found the Silphium in first bloom on 24 July, a week later than usual; during the last six years the average date was 15 July.

When I passed the graveyard again on 3 August, the fence had been removed by a road crew, and the Silphium cut. It is easy now to predict the future; for a few years my Silphium will try in vain to rise above the mowing machine, and then it will die. With it will die the prairie epoch.

The Highway Department says that 100,000 cars pass yearly over this route during the three summer months when the Silphium is in bloom. In them must ride at least 100,000 people who have 'taken' what is called history, and perhaps 25,000 who have 'taken' what is called botany. Yet I doubt whether a dozen have seen the Silphium, and of these hardly one will notice its demise. If I were to tell a preacher of the adjoining church that the road crew has been burning history books in his cemetery, under the guise of mowing weeds, he would be amazed and uncomprehending. How could a weed be a book?

This is one little episode in the funeral of the native flora, which in turn is one episode in the funeral of the floras of the world. Mechanized man, oblivious of floras, is proud of his progress in cleaning up the landscape on which, willy-nilly, he must live out his days. It might be wise to prohibit at once all teaching of real botany and real history, lest some future citizen suffer qualms about the floristic price of his good life.

*　　　　*　　　　*

Thus it comes to pass that farm neighborhoods are good in proportion to the poverty of their floras. My own farm was selected for its lack of goodness and its lack of highway; indeed my whole neighborhood lies in a backwash of the River Progress. My road is the original wagon track of the pioneers, innocent of grades or gravel, brushings or bulldozers. My neighbors bring a sigh to the County Agent. Their fence-rows go unshaven for years on end. Their marshes are neither dyked nor drained. As between going fishing and going forward, they are prone to prefer fishing. Thus on week ends my floristic standard of living is that of the backwoods, while on week days I subsist as best I can on the flora of the university farms, the university campus, and the adjoining suburbs. For a decade I have kept, for pastime, a record of the wild plant species in first bloom on these two diverse areas:

Species First Blooming in	Suburb and Campus	Backward Farm
April	14	26
May	29	59
June	43	70
July	25	56
August	9	14
September	0	1
Total visual diet	120	226

It is apparent that the backward farmer's eye is nearly twice as well fed as the eye of the university student or businessman. Of course neither sees his flora as yet, so we are confronted by the two alternatives already mentioned: either insure the continued blindness of the populace, or examine the question whether we cannot have both progress and plants.

The shrinkage in the flora is due to a combination of clean-farming, woodlot grazing, and good roads. Each of these necessary changes of course requires a larger reduction in the acreage available for wild plants, but none of them requires, or benefits by, the erasure of species from whole farms, townships, or counties. There are idle spots on every farm, and every highway is bordered by an idle strip as long as it is; keep cow, plow, and mower out of these idle spots, and the full native flora, plus dozens of interesting stowaways from foreign parts, could be part of the normal environment of every citizen.

The outstanding conservator of the prairie flora, ironically enough, knows little and cares less about such frivolities: it is the railroad with its fenced right-of-way. Many of these railroad fences were erected before the prairie had been plowed. Within these linear reservations, oblivious of cinders, soot, and annual clean-up fires, the prairie flora still splashes its calendar of colors, from pink shooting-star in May to blue aster in October. I have long wished to confront some hard-boiled railway president with the physical evidence of his soft-heartedness. I have not done so because I haven't met one.

The railroads of course use flame-throwers and chemical sprays to clear the track of weeds, but the cost of such necessary clearance is still too high to extend it much beyond the actual rails. Perhaps further improvements are in the offing.

The erasure of a human subspecies is largely painless—to us—if we know little enough about it. A dead Chinaman is of little import to us whose awareness of things Chinese is bounded by an occasional dish of chow mein. We grieve only for what we know. The erasure of Silphium from western Dane County is no cause for grief if one knows it only as a name in a botany book.

Silphium first became a personality to me when I tried to dig one up to move to my farm. It was like digging an oak sapling. After half an hour of hot grimy labor the root was still enlarging, like a great vertical sweet-potato. As far as I know, that Silphium root went clear through to bedrock. I got no Silphium, but I learned by what elaborate underground stratagems it contrives to weather the prairie drouths.

I next planted Silphium seeds, which are large, meaty, and taste like sunflower seeds. They came up promptly, but after five years of waiting the seedlings are still juvenile, and have not yet borne a flowerstalk. Perhaps it takes a decade for a Silphium to reach

flowering age; how old, then, was my pet plant in the
cemetery? It may have been older than the oldest
tombstone, which is dated 1850. Perhaps it watched
the fugitive Black Hawk retreat from the Madison
lakes to the Wisconsin River; it stood on the route of
that famous march. Certainly it saw the successive
funerals of the local pioneers as they retired, one by
one, to their repose beneath the bluestem.

I once saw a power shovel, while digging a roadside ditch, sever the 'sweet-potato' root of a Silphium
plant. The root soon sprouted new leaves, and eventually it again produced a flower stalk. This explains
why this plant, which never invades new ground, is
nevertheless sometimes seen on recently graded roadsides. Once established, it apparently withstands almost any kind of mutilation except continued grazing,
mowing, or plowing.

Why does Silphium disappear from grazed areas? I
once saw a farmer turn his cows into a virgin prairie
meadow previously used only sporadically for mowing
wild hay. The cows cropped the Silphium to the
ground before any other plant was visibly eaten at all.
One can imagine that the buffalo once had the same

preference for Silphium, but he brooked no fences to confine his nibblings all summer long to one meadow. In short, the buffalo's pasturing was discontinuous, and therefore tolerable to Silphium.

It is a kind providence that has withheld a sense of history from the thousands of species of plants and animals that have exterminated each other to build the present world. The same kind providence now withholds it from us. Few grieved when the last buffalo left Wisconsin, and few will grieve when the last Silphium follows him to the lush prairies of the never-never land.

August

The Green Pasture

SOME PAINTINGS become famous because, being durable, they are viewed by successive generations, in each of which are likely to be found a few appreciative eyes.

I know a painting so evanescent that it is seldom viewed at all, except by some wandering deer. It is a river who wields the brush, and it is the same river who, before I can bring my friends to view his work, erases it forever from human view. After that it exists only in my mind's eye.

Like other artists, my river is temperamental;

there is no predicting when the mood to paint will come upon him, or how long it will last. But in midsummer, when the great white fleets cruise the sky for day after flawless day, it is worth strolling down to the sandbars just to see whether he has been at work.

The work begins with a broad ribbon of silt brushed thinly on the sand of a receding shore. As this dries slowly in the sun, goldfinches bathe in its pools, and deer, herons, kill-deers, raccoons, and turtles cover it with a lacework of tracks. There is no telling, at this stage, whether anything further will happen.

But when I see the silt ribbon turning green with Eleocharis, I watch closely thereafter, for this is the sign that the river is in a painting mood. Almost overnight the Eleocharis becomes a thick turf, so lush and so dense that the meadow mice from the adjoining upland cannot resist the temptation. They move *en masse* to the green pasture, and apparently spend the nights rubbing their ribs in its velvety depths. A maze of neatly tended mouse-trails bespeaks their enthusiasm. The deer walk up and down in it, apparently just for the pleasure of feeling it underfoot. Even a stay-at-home mole has tunneled his way across the dry bar to the Eleocharis ribbon, where he can heave and hump the verdant sod to his heart's content.

At this stage the seedlings of plants too numerous to count and too young to recognize spring to life from the damp warm sand under the green ribbon.

To view the painting, give the river three more weeks of solitude, and then visit the bar on some bright morning just after the sun has melted the daybreak fog. The artist has now laid his colors, and sprayed them with dew. The Eleocharis sod, greener than ever, is now spangled with blue mimulus, pink dragon-head, and the milk-white blooms of Sagittaria. Here and there a cardinal flower thrusts a red spear skyward. At the head of the bar, purple ironweeds and pale pink joe-pyes stand tall against the wall of willows. And if you have come quietly and humbly, as you should to any spot that can be beautiful only once, you may surprise a fox-red deer, standing knee-high in the garden of his delight.

Do not return for a second view of the green pasture, for there is none. Either falling water has dried it out, or rising water has scoured the bar to its original austerity of clean sand. But in your mind you may hang up your picture, and hope that in some other summer the mood to paint may come upon the river.

September

The Choral Copse

By SEPTEMBER, the day breaks with little help from birds. A song sparrow may give a single half-hearted song, a woodcock may twitter overhead *en route* to his daytime thicket, a barred owl may terminate the night's argument with one last wavering call, but few other birds have anything to say or sing about.

It is on some, but not all, of these misty autumn

daybreaks that one may hear the chorus of the quail. The silence is suddenly broken by a dozen contralto voices, no longer able to restrain their praise of the day to come. After a brief minute or two, the music closes as suddenly as it began.

There is a peculiar virtue in the music of elusive birds. Songsters that sing from top-most boughs are easily seen and as easily forgotten; they have the mediocrity of the obvious. What one remembers is the invisible hermit thrush pouring silver chords from impenetrable shadows; the soaring crane trumpeting from behind a cloud; the prairie chicken booming from the mists of nowhere; the quail's Ave Maria in the hush of dawn. No naturalist has even seen the choral act, for the covey is still on its invisible roost in the grass, and any attempt to approach automatically induces silence.

In June it is completely predictable that the robin will give voice when the light intensity reaches 0.01 candle power, and that the bedlam of other singers will follow in predictable sequence. In autumn, on the other hand, the robin is silent, and it is quite unpredictable whether the covey-chorus will occur at all. The disappointment I feel on these mornings of silence perhaps shows that things hoped for have a higher value than things assured. The hope of hearing quail is worth half a dozen risings-in-the-dark.

My farm always has one or more coveys in autumn, but the daybreak chorus is usually distant. I think this is because the coveys prefer to roost as far as possible from the dog, whose interest in quail is even more ardent than my own. One October dawn, however, as I sat sipping coffee by the outdoor fire, a chorus burst into song hardly a stone's throw away. They had roosted under a white-pine copse, possibly to stay dry during the heavy dews.

We felt honored by this daybreak hymn sung almost at our doorstep. Somehow the blue autumnal needles on those pines became thenceforth bluer, and the red carpet of dewberry under those pines became even redder.

October

Smoky Gold

THERE ARE two kinds of hunting: ordinary hunting, and ruffed-grouse hunting.

There are two places to hunt grouse: ordinary places, and Adams County.

There are two times to hunt in Adams: ordinary times, and when the tamaracks are smoky gold. This is written for those luckless ones who have never stood, gun empty and mouth agape, to watch the golden needles come sifting down, while the feathery-rocket that knocked them off sails unscathed into the jackpines.

The tamaracks change from green to yellow when the first frosts have brought woodcock, fox sparrows, and juncos out of the north. Troops of robins are stripping the last white berries from the dogwood thickets, leaving the empty stems as a pink haze against the hill. The creekside alders have shed their leaves, exposing here and there an eyeful of holly. Brambles are aglow, lighting your footsteps grouseward.

The dog knows what is grouseward better than you do. You will do well to follow him closely, reading from the cock of his ears the story the breeze is telling. When at last he stops stock-still, and says with a sideward glance, 'Well, get ready,' the question is, ready for what? A twittering woodcock, or the rising roar of a grouse, or perhaps only a rabbit? In this moment of uncertainty is condensed much of the virtue of grouse hunting. He who must know what to get ready for should go and hunt pheasants.

*   *   *

Hunts differ in flavor, but the reasons are subtle. The sweetest hunts are stolen. To steal a hunt, either go far into the wilderness where no one has been, or else find some undiscovered place under everybody's nose.

Few hunters know that grouse exist in Adams County, for when they drive through it, they see only a waste of jackpines and scrub oaks. This is because the highway intersects a series of west-running creeks, each of which heads in a swamp, but drops to the river through dry sand-barrens. Naturally the northbound highway intersects these swampless barrens, but just above the highway, and behind the screen of dry scrub, every creeklet expands into a broad ribbon of swamp, a sure haven for grouse.

Here, come October, I sit in the solitude of my tamaracks and hear the hunters' cars roaring up the highway, hell-bent for the crowded counties to the north.

I chuckle as I picture their dancing speedometers, their strained faces, their eager eyes glued on the northward horizon. At the noise of their passing, a cock grouse drums his defiance. My dog grins as we note his direction. That fellow, we agree, needs some exercise; we shall look him up presently.

The tamaracks grow not only in the swamp, but at the foot of the bordering upland, where springs break forth. Each spring has become choked with moss, which forms a boggy terrace. I call these terraces the hanging gardens, for out of their sodden muck the fringed gentians have lifted blue jewels. Such an October gentian, dusted with tamarack gold, is worth a full stop and a long look, even when the dog signals grouse ahead.

Between each hanging garden and the creekside is a moss-paved deer trail, handy for the hunter to follow, and for the flushed grouse to cross—in a split second. The question is whether the bird and the gun agree on how a second should be split. If they do not, the next deer that passes finds a pair of empty shells to sniff at, but no feathers.

Higher up the creeklet I encounter an abandoned farm. I try to read, from the age of the young jackpines marching across an old field, how long ago the luckless farmer found out that sand plains were meant to grow solitude, not corn. Jackpines tell tall tales to the unwary, for they put on several whorls of branches each year, instead of only one. I find a better chronometer in an elm seedling that now blocks the barn door. Its rings date back to the drouth of 1930. Since that year no man has carried milk out of this barn.

I wonder what this family thought about when their mortgage finally outgrew their crops, and thus gave the signal for their eviction. Many thoughts, like flying grouse, leave no trace of their passing, but some leave clues that outlast the decades. He who, in some unforgotten April, planted this lilac must have thought pleasantly of blooms for all the Aprils to come. She who used this washboard, its corrugations worn thin with many Mondays, may have wished for a cessation of all Mondays, and soon.

Musing on such questions, I become aware of the dog down by the spring, pointing patiently these many minutes. I walk up, apologizing for my inattention. Up twitters a woodcock, batlike, his salmon breast soaked in October sun. Thus goes the hunt.

It's hard on such a day to keep one's mind on grouse, for there are many distractions. I cross a buck track in the sand, and follow in idle curiosity. The track leads straight from one Jersey tea bush to another, with nipped twigs showing why.

This reminds me of my own lunch, but before I get it pulled out of my game pocket, I see a circling hawk, high skyward, needing identification. I wait till he banks and shows his red tail.

I reach again for the lunch, but my eye catches a peeled popple. Here a buck has rubbed off his itchy velvet. How long ago? The exposed wood is already brown; I conclude that horns must therefore be clean by now.

I reach again for the lunch, but am interrupted by an excited yawp from the dog, and a crash of bushes in the swamp. Out springs a buck, flag aloft, horns shining, his coat a sleek blue. Yes, the popple told the truth.

This time I get the lunch all the way out and sit down to eat. A chickadee watches me, and grows confidential about *his* lunch. He doesn't say what he ate, perhaps it was cool turgid ant-eggs, or some other avian equivalent of cold roast grouse.

Lunch over, I regard a phalanx of young tamaracks, their golden lances thrusting skyward. Under each the needles of yesterday fall to earth building a blanket of smoky gold; at the tip of each the bud of tomorrow, preformed, poised, awaits another spring.

Too Early

Getting up too early is a vice habitual in horned owls, stars, geese, and freight trains. Some hunters acquire it from geese, and some coffee pots from hunters. It

is strange that of all the multitude of creatures who must rise in the morning at some time, only these few should have discovered the most pleasant and least useful time for doing it.

Orion must have been the original mentor of the too-early company, for it is he who signals for too-early rising. It is time when Orion has passed west of the zenith about as far as one should lead a teal.

Early risers feel at ease with each other, perhaps because, unlike those who sleep late, they are given to understatement of their own achievements. Orion, the most widely traveled, says literally nothing. The coffee pot, from its first soft gurgle, underclaims the virtues of what simmers within. The owl, in his trisyllabic commentary, plays down the story of the night's murders. The goose on the bar, rising briefly to a point of order in some inaudible anserine debate, lets fall no hint that he speaks with the authority of all the far hills and the sea.

The freight, I admit, is hardly reticent about his own importance, yet even he has a kind of modesty:

his eye is single to his own noisy business, and he never comes roaring into somebody else's camp. I feel a deep security in this single-mindedness of freight trains.

*   *   *   *

To arrive too early in the marsh is an adventure in pure listening; the ear roams at will among the noises of the night, without let or hindrance from hand or eye. When you hear a mallard being audibly enthusiastic about his soup, you are free to picture a score guzzling among the duckweeds. When one widgeon squeals, you may postulate a squadron without fear of visual contradiction. And when a flock of bluebills, pitching pondward, tears the dark silk of heaven in one long rending nose-dive, you catch your breath at the sound, but there is nothing to see except stars. This same performance, in daytime, would have to be looked at, shot at, missed, and then hurriedly fitted with an alibi. Nor could daylight add anything to your mind's eye picture of quivering wings, ripping the firmament neatly into halves.

The hour of listening ends when the fowl depart on muted wings for wider safer waters, each flock a blur against the graying east.

Like many another treaty of restraint, the pre-dawn pact lasts only as long as darkness humbles the arrogant. It would seem as if the sun were responsible for the daily retreat of reticence from the world. At any rate, by the time the mists are white over the lowlands, every rooster is bragging *ad lib*, and every corn shock is pretending to be twice as tall as any corn that ever grew. By sun-up every squirrel is exaggerating some fancied indignity to his person, and every jaw proclaiming with false emotion about supposititious dangers to society, at this very moment discovered by him. Distant crows are berating a hypothetical owl, just to tell the world how vigilant crows are, and a pheasant cock, musing perhaps on his philanderings of bygone days, beats the air with his wings and tells the world in raucous warning that he owns this marsh and all the hens in it.

Nor are all these illusions of grandeur confined to the birds and beasts. By breakfast time come the honks, horns, shouts, and whistles of the awakened farmyard, and finally, at evening, the drone of an untended radio. Then everybody goes to bed to relearn the lessons of the night.

Red Lanterns

One way to hunt partridge is to make a plan, based on logic and probabilities, of the terrain to be hunted. This will take you over the ground where the birds ought to be.

Another way is to wander, quite aimlessly, from one red lantern to another. This will likely take you where the birds actually are. The lanterns are blackberry leaves, red in October sun.

Red lanterns have lighted my way on many a pleasant hunt in many a region, but I think that blackberries must first have learned how to glow in the sand counties of central Wisconsin. Along the little boggy streams of these friendly wastes, called poor by those whose own lights barely flicker, the blackberries burn richly red on every sunny day from first frost to the last day of the season. Every woodcock and every partridge has his private solarium under these briars. Most hunters, not knowing this, wear themselves out in the briarless scrub, and, returning home birdless, leave the rest of us in peace.

By 'us' I mean the birds, the stream, the dog, and myself. The stream is a lazy one; he winds through the alders as if he would rather stay here than reach the river. So would I. Every one of his hairpin hesitations means that much more streambank where hillside briars adjoin dank beds of frozen ferns and jewelweeds on the boggy bottom. No partridge can long absent himself from such a place, nor can I. Partridge hunting, then, is a creekside stroll, upwind, from one briar patch to another.

The dog, when he approaches the briars, looks around to make sure I am within gunshot. Reassured, he advances with stealthy caution, his wet nose screening a hundred scents for that one scent, the potential presence of which gives life and meaning to the whole landscape. He is the prospector of the air, perpetually searching its strata for olfactory gold. Partridge scent is the gold standard that relates his world to mine.

My dog, by the way, thinks I have much to learn about partridges, and, being a professional naturalist, I agree. He persists in tutoring me, with the calm patience of a professor of logic, in the art of drawing deductions from an educated nose. I delight in seeing him deduce a conclusion, in the form of a point, from data that are obvious to him, but speculative to my unaided eye. Perhaps he hopes his dull pupil will one day learn to smell.

Like other dull pupils, I know when the professor is right, even though I do not know why. I check my gun and walk in. Like any good professor, the dog never laughs when I miss, which is often. He gives me just one look, and proceeds up the stream in quest of another grouse.

Following one of these banks, one walks astride two landscapes, the hillside one hunts from, and the bottom the dog hunts in. There is a special charm in treading soft dry carpets of Lycopodium to flush birds out of the bog, and the first test of a partridge dog is his willingness to do the wet work while you parallel him on the dry bank.

A special problem arises where the belt of alders widens, and the dog disappears from view. Hurry at once to a knoll or point, where you stand stock-still, straining eye and ear to follow the dog. A sudden scattering of whitethroats may reveal his whereabouts. Again you may hear him breaking a twig, or splashing in a wet spot, or plopping into the creek. But when all sound ceases, be ready for instant action, for he is likely on point. Listen now for the premonitory clucks a frightened partridge gives just before flushing. Then follows the hurtling bird, or perhaps two of them, or I have known as many as six, clucking and flushing one by one, each sailing high for his own destination in the uplands. Whether one passes within gunshot is of course a matter of chance, and you can compute the chance if you have time: 360 degrees divided by 30, or whatever segment of the circle your gun covers. Divide again by 3 or 4, which is your chance of missing, and you have the probability of actual feathers in the hunting coat.

The second test of a good partridge dog is whether he reports for orders after such an episode. Sit down and talk it over with him while he pants. Then look for the next red lantern, and proceed with the hunt.

The October breeze brings my dog many scents other than grouse, each of which may lead to its own peculiar episode. When he points with a certain humorous expression of the ears, I know he has found a bedded rabbit. Once a dead-serious point yielded no bird, but still the dog stood frozen; in a tuft of sedge under his very nose was a fat sleeping coon, getting his share of October sun. At least once on each hunt the dog bays a skunk, usually in some denser-than-ordinary thicket of blackberries. Once the dog pointed in midstream: a whir of wings upriver, followed by three musical cries, told me he had interrupted a wood duck's dinner. Not infrequently he finds jacksnipe in heavily pastured alders, and lastly he may put out a deer, bedded for the day on a high streambank flanked by alder bog. Has the deer a poetical weakness for singing waters, or a practical liking for a bed that cannot be approached without making a noise? Judging by the indignant flick of his great white flag it might be either, or both.

Almost anything may happen between one red lantern and another.

*　　　*　　　*

At sunset on the last day of the grouse season, every blackberry blows out his light. I do not understand how a mere bush can thus be infallibly informed about the Wisconsin statutes, nor have I ever gone back next day to find out. For the ensuing eleven months the lanterns glow only in recollection. I sometimes think that the other months were constituted mainly as a fitting interlude between Octobers, and I suspect that dogs, and perhaps grouse, share the same view.

November

If I Were the Wind

THE WIND that makes music in November corn is in a hurry. The stalks hum, the loose husks whisk skyward in half-playful swirls, and the wind hurries on.

In the marsh, long windy waves surge across the grassy sloughs, beat against the far willows. A tree tries to argue, bare limbs waving, but there is no detaining the wind.

On the sandbar there is only wind, and the river sliding seaward. Every wisp of grass is drawing circles on the sand. I wander over the bar to a driftwood log, where I sit and listen to the universal roar, and to the tinkle of wavelets on the shore. The river is lifeless: not a duck, heron, marshhawk, or gull but has sought refuge from wind.

*   *   *

Out of the clouds I hear a faint bark, as of a faraway dog. It is strange how the world cocks its ears at that sound, wondering. Soon it is louder: the honk of geese, invisible, but coming on.

The flock emerges from the low clouds, a tattered banner of birds, dipping and rising, blown up and blown down, blown together and blown apart, but advancing, the wind wrestling lovingly with each winnowing wing. When the flock is a blur in the far sky I hear the last honk, sounding taps for summer.

*   *   *

It is warm behind the driftwood now, for the wind has gone with the geese. So would I—if I were the wind.

Axe-in-Hand

The Lord giveth, and the Lord taketh away, but He is no longer the only one to do so. When some remote ancestor of ours invented the shovel, he became a giver: he could plant a tree. And when the axe was invented, he became a taker: he could chop it down. Whoever owns land has thus assumed, whether he knows it or not, the divine functions of creating and destroying plants.

Other ancestors, less remote, have since invented other tools, but each of these, upon close scrutiny, proves to be either an elaboration of, or an accessory to, the original pair of basic implements. We classify ourselves into vocations, each of which either wields some particular tool, or sells it, or repairs it, or sharpens it, or dispenses advice on how to do so; by such division of labors we avoid responsibility for the misuse of any tool save our own. But there is one vocation—philosophy—which knows that all men, by what they think about and wish for, in effect wield all tools. It knows that men thus determine, by their manner of thinking and wishing, whether it is worth while to wield any.

*   *   *

November is, for many reasons, the month for the axe. It is warm enough to grind an axe without freezing, but cold enough to fell a tree in comfort. The leaves are off the hardwoods, so that one can see just how the branches intertwine, and what growth occurred last summer. Without this clear view of treetops, one cannot be sure which tree, if any, needs felling for the good of the land.

I have read many definitions of what is a conservationist, and written not a few myself, but I suspect that the best one is written not with a pen, but with an axe. It is a matter of what a man thinks about while chopping, or while deciding what to chop. A conservationist is one who is humbly aware that with each stroke he is writing his signature on the face of his land. Signatures of course differ, whether written with axe or pen, and this is as it should be.

I find it disconcerting to analyze, *ex post facto*, the reasons behind my own axe-in-hand decisions. I find, first of all, that not all trees are created free and equal. Where a white pine and a red birch are crowding each other, I have an *a priori* bias; I always cut the birch to favor the pine. Why?

Well, first of all, I planted the pine with my shovel, whereas the birch crawled in under the fence and planted itself. My bias is thus to some extent paternal, but this cannot be the whole story, for if the pine were a natural seedling like the birch, I would value it even more. So I must dig deeper for the logic, if any, behind my bias.

The birch is an abundant tree in my township and becoming more so, whereas pine is scarce and becoming scarcer; perhaps my bias is for the underdog. But, what would I do if my farm were further north, where pine is abundant and red birch is scarce? I confess I don't know. My farm is here.

The pine will live for a century, the birch for half that; do I fear that my signature will fade? My neighbors have planted no pines but all have many birches; am I snobbish about having a woodlot of distinction? The pine stays green all winter, the birch punches the clock in October; do I favor the tree that, like myself, braves the winter wind? The pine will shelter a grouse but the birch will feed him; do I consider bed more important than board? The pine will ultimately bring ten dollars a thousand, the birch two dollars; have I an eye on the bank? All of these possible reasons for my bias seem to carry some weight, but none of them carries very much.

So I try again, and here perhaps is something; under this pine will ultimately grow a trailing arbutus, an Indian pipe, a pyrola, or a twin flower, whereas under the birch a bottle gentian is about the best to be hoped for. In this pine a pileated woodpecker will ultimately chisel out a nest; in the birch a hairy will have to suffice. In this pine the wind will sing for me in April, at which time the birch is only rattling naked twigs. These possible reasons for my bias carry weight, but why? Does the pine stimulate my imagination and my hopes more deeply than the birch does? If so, is the difference in the trees, or in me?

The only conclusion I have ever reached is that I love all trees, but I am in love with pines.

As I said, November is the month for the axe, and, as in other love affairs, there is skill in the exercise of bias. If the birch stands south of the pine, and is taller, it will shade the pine's leader in the spring, and thus discourage the pine weevil from laying her eggs there. Birch competition is a minor affliction compared with this weevil, whose progeny kill the pine's leader and thus deform the tree. It is interesting to meditate that this insect's preference for squatting in the sun determines not only her own continuity as a species, but also the future figure of my pine, and my own success as a wielder of axe and shovel.

Again, if a drouthy summer follows my removal of the birch's shade, the hotter soil may offset the lesser competition for water, and my pine be none the better for my bias.

Lastly, if the birch's limbs rub the pine's terminal buds during a wind, the pine will surely be deformed, and the birch must either be removed regardless of other considerations, or else it must be pruned of limbs each winter to a height greater than the pine's prospective summer growth.

Such are the pros and cons the wielder of an axe must foresee, compare, and decide upon with the calm assurance that his bias will, on the average, prove to be something more than good intentions.

The wielder of an axe has as many biases as there are species of trees on his farm. In the course of the years he imputes to each species, from his responses to their beauty or utility, and their responses to his labors for or against them, a series of attributes that constitute a character. I am amazed to learn what diverse characters different men impute to one and the same tree.

Thus to me the aspen is in good repute because he glorifies October and he feeds my grouse in winter, but to some of my neighbors he is a mere weed, perhaps because he sprouted so vigorously in the stump lots their grandfathers were attempting to clear. (I cannot sneer at this, for I find myself disliking the elms whose resproutings threaten my pines.)

Again, the tamarack is to me a favorite second only to white pine, perhaps because he is nearly extinct in my township (underdog bias), or because he sprinkles gold on October grouse (gunpowder bias), or because he sours the soil and enables it to grow the loveliest of our orchids, the showy lady's-slipper. On the other hand, foresters have excommunicated the tamarack because he grows too slowly to pay compound interest. In order to clinch this dispute, they also mention that he succumbs periodically to epizootics of saw-fly, but this is fifty years hence for my tamaracks, so I shall let my grandson worry about it. Meanwhile my tamaracks are growing so lustily that my spirits soar with them, skyward.

To me an ancient cottonwood is the greatest of trees because in his youth he shaded the buffalo and wore a halo of pigeons, and I like a young cottonwood because he may some day become ancient. But the farmer's wife (and hence the farmer) despises all cottonwoods because in June the female tree clogs the screens with cotton. The modern dogma is comfort at any cost.

I find my biases more numerous than those of my neighbors because I have individual likings for many species that they lump under one aspersive category: brush. Thus I like the wahoo, partly because deer, rabbits, and mice are so avid to eat his square twigs and green bark and partly because his cerise berries glow so warmly against November snow. I like the red dogwood because he feeds October robins, and the prickly ash because my woodcock take their daily sunbath under the shelter of his thorns. I like the hazel because his October purple feeds my eye, and because his November catkins feed my deer and grouse. I like the bitter-sweet because my father did, and because the deer, on the 1st of July of each year, begin suddenly to eat the new leaves, and I have learned to predict this event to my guests. I cannot dislike a plant that enables me, a mere professor, to blossom forth annually as a successful seer and prophet.

It is evident that our plant biases are in part traditional. If your grandfather liked hickory nuts, you will like the hickory tree because your father told you to. If, on the other hand, your grandfather burned a log carrying a poison ivy vine and recklessly stood in the smoke, you will dislike the species, no matter with what crimson glories it warms your eyes each fall.

It is also evident that our plant biases reflect not only vocations but avocations, with a delicate allocation of priority as between industry and indolence. The farmer who would rather hunt grouse than milk cows will not dislike hawthorn, no matter if it does invade his pasture. The coon-hunter will not dislike basswood, and I know of quail hunters who bear no grudge against ragweed, despite their annual bout with hayfever. Our biases are indeed a sensitive index to our affections, our tastes, our loyalties, our generosities, and our manner of wasting weekends.

Be that as it may, I am content to waste mine, in November, with axe in hand.

A Mighty Fortress

Every farm woodland, in addition to yielding lumber, fuel, and posts, should provide its owner a liberal education. This crop of wisdom never fails, but it is not always harvested. I here record some of the many lessons I have learned in my own woods.

*   *   *

Soon after I bought the woods a decade ago, I realized that I had bought almost as many tree diseases as I had trees. My woodlot is riddled by all the ailments wood is heir to. I began to wish that Noah, when he loaded up the Ark, had left the tree diseases behind. But it soon became clear that these same diseases made my woodlot a mighty fortress, unequaled in the whole county.

My woods is headquarters for a family of coons; few of my neighbors have any. One Sunday in November, after a new snow, I learned why. The fresh track of a coon-hunter and his hound led up to a half-uprooted maple, under which one of my coons had taken refuge. The frozen snarl of roots and earth was too rocky to chop and too tough to dig; the holes under the roots were too numerous to smoke out. The hunter had quit coonless because a fungus disease had weakened the roots of the maple. The tree, half tipped over by a storm, offers an impregnable fortress for coondom. Without this 'bombproof' shelter, my seed stock of coons would be cleaned out by hunters each year.

My woods houses a dozen ruffed grouse, but during periods of deep snow my grouse shift to my neighbor's woods, where there is better cover. However, I always retain as many grouse as I have oaks wind-thrown by summer storms. These summer windfalls keep their dried leaves, and during snows each such windfall harbors a grouse. The droppings show that each grouse roosts, feeds, and loafs for the duration of the storm within the narrow confines of his leafy camouflage, safe from wind, owl, fox, and hunter. The cured oak leaves not only serve as cover, but, for some curious reason, are relished as food by the grouse.

These oak windfalls are, of course, diseased trees. Without disease, few oaks would break off, and hence few grouse would have down tops to hide in.

Diseased oaks also provide another apparently delectable grouse food: oak galls. A gall is a diseased growth of new twigs that have been stung by a gall-wasp while tender and succulent. In October my grouse are often stuffed with oak galls.

Each year the wild bees load up one of my hollow oaks with combs, and each year trespassing honey-hunters harvest the honey before I do. This is partly because they are more skillful than I am in 'lining up' the bee trees, and partly because they use nets, and hence are able to work before the bees become dormant in fall. But for heart-rots, there would be no hollow oaks to furnish wild bees with oaken hives.

During high years of the cycle, there is a plague of rabbits in my woods. They eat the bark and twigs off almost every kind of tree or bush I am trying to encourage, and ignore almost every kind I should like to have less of. (When the rabbit-hunter plants himself a grove of pines or an orchard, the rabbit somehow ceases to be a game animal and becomes a pest instead.)

The rabbit, despite his omnivorous appetite, is an epicure in some respects. He always prefers a hand-planted pine, maple, apple, or wahoo to a wild one.

CHARLES W.
SCHWARTZ

He also insists that certain salads be preconditioned before he deigns to eat them. Thus he spurns red dogwood until it is attacked by oyster-shell scale, after which the bark becomes a delicacy, to be eagerly devoured by all the rabbits in the neighborhood.

A flock of a dozen chickadees spends the year in my woods. In winter, when we are harvesting diseased or dead trees for our fuel wood, the ring of the axe is dinner gong for the chickadee tribe. They hang in the offing waiting for the tree to fall, offering pert commentary on the slowness of our labor. When the tree at last is down, and the wedges begin to open up its contents, the chickadees draw up their white napkins and fall to. Every slab of dead bark is, to them, a treasury of eggs, larvae, and cocoons. For them every ant-tunneled heartwood bulges with milk and honey. We often stand a fresh split against a near-by tree just to see the greedy chicks mop up the ant-eggs. It lightens our labor to know that they, as well as we, derive aid and comfort from the fragrant riches of newly split oak.

But for diseases and insect pests, there would likely be no food in these trees, and hence no chickadees to add cheer to my woods in winter.

Many other kinds of wildlife depend on tree diseases. My pileated woodpeckers chisel living pines, to extract fat grubs from the diseased heartwood. My barred owls find surcease from crows and jays in the hollow heart of an old basswood; but for this diseased tree their sundown serenade would probably be silenced. My wood ducks nest in hollow trees; every June brings its brood of downy ducklings to my woodland slough. All squirrels depend, for permanent dens, on a delicately balanced equilibrium between a rotting cavity and the scar tissue with which the tree attempts to close the wound. The squirrels referee the contest by gnawing out the scar tissue when it begins unduly to shrink the amplitude of their front door.

The real jewel of my disease-ridden woodlot is the prothonotary warbler. He nests in an old woodpecker hole, or other small cavity, in a dead snag overhanging water. The flash of his gold-and-blue plumage amid the dank decay of the June woods is in itself proof that dead trees are transmuted into living animals, and vice versa. When you doubt the wisdom of this arrangement, take a look at the prothonotary.

December

Home Range

THE WILD things that live on my farm are reluctant to tell me, in so many words, how much of my township is included within their daily or nightly beat. I am curious about this, for it gives me the ratio between the size of their universe and the size of mine, and it conveniently begs the much more important question, who is the more thoroughly acquainted with the world in which he lives?

Like people, my animals frequently disclose by their actions what they decline to divulge in words. It is difficult to predict when and how one of these disclosures will come to light.

*   *   *

The dog, being no hand with an axe, is free to hunt while the rest of us are making wood. A sudden *yip-yip-yip* gives us notice that a rabbit, flushed from his bed in the grass, is headed elsewhere in a hurry. He makes a beeline for a woodpile a quarter-mile distant, where he ducks between two corded stacks, a safe gunshot ahead of his pursuer. The dog, after leaving a few symbolic toothmarks on the hard oak, gives it up and resumes his search for some less canny cotton-tail, and we resume our chopping.

This little episode tells me that this rabbit is fami-liar with all of the ground between his bed in the meadow and his blitz-cellar under the woodpile. How else the beeline? This rabbit's home range is at least a quarter-mile in extent.

The chickadees that visit our feeding station are trapped and banded each winter. Some of our neigh-bors also feed chickadees, but none band them. By noticing the furthest points from my feeder at which banded chickadees are seen, we have learned that the home range of our flock is half a mile across in winter, but that it includes only areas protected from wind.

In summer, when the flock has dispersed for nest-ing, banded birds are seen at greater distances, often mated with unbanded birds. At this season the chick-adees pay no heed to wind, often being found in open wind-swept places.

The fresh tracks of three deer, clear in yesterday's snow, pass through our woods. I follow the tracks backward and find a cluster of three beds, clear of snow, in the big willow thicket on the sandbar.

I then follow the tracks forward; they lead to my neighbor's cornfield, where the deer have pawed waste corn out of the snow, and also tousled one of the shocks. The tracks then lead back, by another route, to the sandbar. *En route* the deer have pawed at some grass tufts, nuzzling for the tender green sprouts within, and they have also drunk at a spring. My picture of the night's routine is complete. The over-all distance from bed to breakfast is a mile.

Our woods always harbors grouse, but one day last

winter, after a deep and soft snow, I could find neither a grouse nor a track of one. I had about concluded that my birds had moved out, when my dog came to a point in the leafy top of an oak blown down last summer. Three grouse flushed out, one by one.

There were no tracks under or near the down top. Obviously threse birds had flown in, but from where? Grouse must eat, especially in zero weather, so I examined the droppings for a clue. Among much unrecognizable debris I found bud-scales, and also the tough yellow skins of frozen nightshade berries.

In a thicket of young soft maple I had noticed, in summer, an abundant growth of nightshade. I went there and, after a search, found grouse tracks on a log. The birds had not waded the soft snow; they had walked the logs and picked the berries projecting here and there within their reach. This was a quartermile east of the down oak.

That evening, at sunset, I saw a grouse budding in

a popple thicket a quarter-mile west. There were no tracks. This completed the story. These birds, for the duration of the soft snow, were covering their home range a-wing, not afoot, and the range was half a mile across.

*   *   *

Science knows little about home range: how big it is at various seasons, what food and cover it must include, when and how it is defended against trespass, and whether ownership is an individual, family, or group affair. These are the fundamentals of animal economics, or ecology. Every farm is a textbook on animal ecology; woodsmanship is the translation of the book.

Pines Above the Snow

Acts of creation are ordinarily reserved for gods and poets, but humbler folk may circumvent this restriction if they know how. To plant a pine, for example, one need be neither god nor poet; one need only own a shovel. By virtue of this curious loophole in the rules, any clodhopper may say: Let there be a tree—and there will be one.

If his back be strong and his shovel sharp, there may eventually be ten thousand. And in the seventh year he may lean upon his shovel, and look upon his trees, and find them good.

God passed on his handiwork as early as the seventh day, but I notice He has since been rather noncommittal about its merits. I gather either that He spoke too soon, or that trees stand more looking upon than do fig leaves and firmaments.

*   *   *

Why is the shovel regarded as a symbol of drudgery? Perhaps because most shovels are dull. Certainly all drudges have dull shovels, but I am uncertain which of these two facts is cause and which effect. I only know that a good file, vigorously wielded, makes my shovel sing as it slices the mellow loam. I am told there is music in the sharp plane, the sharp chisel, and the sharp scalpel, but I hear it best in my shovel; it hums in my wrists as I plant a pine. I suspect that the fellow who tried so hard to strike one clear note upon the harp of time chose too difficult an instrument.

It is well that the planting season comes only in spring, for moderation is best in all things, even shovels. During the other months you may watch the process of becoming a pine.

The pine's new year begins in May, when the terminal bud becomes 'the candle.' Whoever coined that name for the new growth had subtlety in his soul. 'The candle' sounds like a platitudinous reference to obvious facts: the new shoot is waxy, upright, brittle. But he who lives with pines knows that candle has a deeper meaning, for at its tip burns the eternal flame that lights a path into the future. May after May my pines follow their candles skyward, each headed straight for the zenith, and each meaning to get there if only there be years enough before the last trumpet blows. It is a very old pine who at last forgets which of his many candles is the most important, and thus flattens his crown against the sky. You may forget, but no pine of your own planting will do so in your lifetime.

If you are thriftily inclined, you will find pines congenial company, for, unlike the hand-to-mouth hardwoods, they never pay current bills out of current earnings; they live solely on their savings of the year before. In fact every pine carries an open bankbook, in which his cash balance is recorded by 30 June of each year. If, on that date, his completed candle has developed a terminal cluster of ten or twelve buds, it means that he has salted away enough rain and sun for a two-foot or even a three-foot thrust skyward next spring. If there are only four to six buds, his thrust will be a lesser one, but he will nevertheless wear that peculiar air that goes with solvency.

Hard years, of course, come to pines as they do to men, and these are recorded as shorter thrusts, i.e. shorter spaces between the successive whorls of branches. These spaces, then, are an autobiography that he who walks with trees may read at will. In order to date a hard year correctly, you must always subtract one from the year of lesser growth. Thus the 1937 growth was short in all pines; this records the universal drouth of 1936. On the other hand the 1941 growth was long in all pines; perhaps they saw the shadow of things to come, and made a special effort to show the world that pines still know where they are going, even though men do not.

When one pine shows a short year but his neighbors do not, you may safely interpolate some purely local or individual adversity: a fire scar, a gnawing meadowmouse, a windburn, or some local bottleneck in that dark laboratory we call the soil.

*   *   *

There is much small-talk and neighborhood gossip among pines. By paying heed to this chatter, I learn what has transpired during the week when I am absent in town. Thus in March, when the deer frequently browse white pines, the height of the browsings tells me how hungry they are. A deer full of corn is too lazy to nip branches more than four feet above the ground; a really hungry deer rises on his hind legs and nips as high as eight feet. Thus I learn the gastronomic status of the deer without seeing them, and I learn, without visiting his field, whether my neighbor has hauled in his cornshocks.

In May, when the new candle is tender and brittle as an asparagus shoot, a bird alighting on it will often break it off. Every spring I find a few such decapitated trees, each with its wilted candle lying in the grass. It is easy to infer what has happened, but in a decade of watching I have never once *seen* a bird break a candle. It is an object lesson: one need not doubt the unseen.

In June of each year a few white pines suddenly show wilted candles, which shortly thereafter turn brown and die. A pine weevil has bored into the terminal bud cluster and deposited eggs; the grubs, when hatched, bore down along the pith and kill the shoot. Such a leaderless pine is doomed to frustration, for the surviving branches disagree among themselves who is to head the skyward march. They all do, and as a consequence the tree remains a bush.

It is a curious circumstance that only pines in full sunlight are bitten by weevils; shaded pines are ignored. Such are the hidden uses of adversity.

In October my pines tell me, by their rubbed-off bark, when the bucks are beginning to 'feel their oats.' A jackpine about eight feet high, and standing alone, seems especially to incite in a buck the idea that the world needs prodding. Such a tree must perforce turn the other cheek also, and emerges much the worse for wear. The only element of justice in such combats is that the more the tree is punished, the more pitch the buck carries away on his not-so-shiny antlers.

The chit-chat of the woods is sometimes hard to translate. Once in midwinter I found in the droppings under a grouse roost some half-digested structures that I could not identify. They resembled miniature corncobs about half an inch long. I examined samples of every local grouse food I could think of, but without finding any clue to the origin of the 'cobs.' Finally I cut open the terminal bud of a jackpine, and in its core I found the answer. The grouse had eaten the buds, digested the pitch, rubbed off the scales in his gizzard, and left the cob, which was, in effect, the forthcoming candle. One might say that this grouse had been speculating in jackpine 'futures.'

*   *   *

The three species of pine native to Wisconsin (white, red, and jack) differ radically in their opinions about marriageable age. The precocious jackpine sometimes blooms and bears cones a year or two after leaving the nursery, and a few of my 13-year-old jacks already boast of grandchildren. My 13-year-old reds first bloomed this year, but my whites have not yet bloomed; they adhere closely to the Anglo-Saxon doctrine of free, white, and twenty-one.

Were it not for this wide diversity in social outlook, my red squirrels would be much curtailed in their bill-of-fare. Each year in midsummer they start tearing up jackpine cones for the seeds, and no Labor-Day picnic ever scattered more hulls and rinds over the landscape than they do: under each tree the remains of their annual feast lie in piles and heaps. Yet there are always cones to spare, as attested by their progeny popping up among the gold-enrods.

Few people know that pines bear flowers, and most of those who do are too prosy to see in this festival of bloom anything more than a routine biological function. All disillusioned folk should spend the second week in May in a pine woods, and such as wear glasses should take along an extra handkerchief. The prodigality of pine pollen should convince anyone of the reckless exuberance of the season, even when the song of the kinglet has failed to do so.

Young white pines usually thrive best in the absence of their parents. I know of whole woodlots in which the younger generation, even when provided with a place in the sun, is dwarfed and spindled by its elders. Again there are woodlots in which no such inhibition obtains. I wish I knew whether such differences lie in tolerance in the young, in the old, or in the soil.

Pines, like people, are choosy about their associates and do not succeed in suppressing their likes and dislikes. Thus there is an affinity between white pines and dewberries, between red pines and flowering spurge, between jackpines and sweet fern. When I plant a white pine in a dewberry patch, I can safely predict that within a year he will develop a husky cluster of buds, and that his new needles will show that bluish bloom which bespeaks health and congenial company. He will outgrow and outbloom his fellows planted on the same day, with the same care, in the same soil, but in the company of grass.

In October I like to walk among these blue plumes, rising straight and stalwart from the red carpet of dewberry leaves. I wonder whether they are aware of their state of well-being. I know only that I am.

Pines have earned the reputation of being 'evergreen' by the same device that governments use to achieve the appearance of perpetuity: overlapping terms of office. By taking on new needles on the new growth of each year, and discarding old needles at longer intervals, they have led the casual onlooker to believe that needles remain forever green.

Each species of pine has its own constitution, which prescribes a term of office for needles appropriate to its way of life. Thus the white pine retains its needles for a year and a half; the red and jackpines for two years and a half. Incoming needles take office in June, and outgoing needles write farewell addresses in October. All write the same thing, in the same tawny yellow ink, which by November turns brown. Then the needles fall, and are filed in the duff to enrich the wisdom of the stand. It is this accumulated wisdom that hushes the footsteps of whoever walks under pines.

It is in midwinter that I sometimes glean from my pines something more important than woodlot politics, and the news of the wind and weather. This is especially likely to happen on some gloomy evening when the snow has buried all irrelevant detail, and the hush of elemental sadness lies heavy upon every living thing. Nevertheless, my pines, each with his burden of snow, are standing ramrod-straight, rank upon rank, and in the dusk beyond I sense the presence of hundreds more. At such times I feel a curious transfusion of courage.

65290

To band a bird is to hold a ticket in a great lottery. Most of us hold tickets on our own survival, but we buy them from the insurance company, which knows too much to sell us a really sporting chance. It is an exercise in objectivity to hold a ticket on the banded sparrow that falleth, or on the banded chickadee that may some day re-enter your trap, and thus prove that he is still alive.

The tyro gets his thrill from banding new birds; he plays a kind of game against himself, striving to break his previous score for total numbers. But to the old-timer the banding of new birds becomes merely pleasant routine; the real thrill lies in the recapture of some bird banded long ago, some bird whose age, adventures, and previous condition of appetite are perhaps better known to you than to the bird himself.

Thus in our family, the question whether chickadee 65290 would survive for still another winter was, for five years, a sporting question of the first magnitude.

Beginning a decade ago, we have trapped and banded most of the chickadees on our farm each winter. In early winter, the traps yield mostly unbanded birds; these presumably are mostly the young of the year, which, once banded, can thereafter be 'dated.' As the winter wears on, unbanded birds cease to appear in the trap; we then know that the local population consists largely of marked birds. We can tell from the band numbers how many birds are present, and how many of these are survivors from each previous year of banding.

65290 was one of 7 chickadees constituting the 'class of 1937.' When he first entered our trap, he showed no visible evidence of genius. Like his classmates, his valor for suet was greater than his discretion. Like his classmates, he bit my finger while being taken out of the trap. When banded and released he fluttered up to a limb, pecked his new aluminum anklet in mild annoyance, shook his mussed feathers, cursed gently, and hurried away to catch up with the gang. It is doubtful whether he drew any philosophical deductions from his experience (such as 'all is not ants' eggs that glitters'), for he was caught again three times that same winter.

By the second winter our recaptures showed that the class of 7 had shrunk to 3, and by the third winter to 2. By the fifth winter 65290 was the sole survivor of his generation. Signs of genius were still lacking, but of his extraordinary capacity for living, there was now historical proof.

During his sixth winter 65290 failed to reappear, and the verdict of 'missing in action' is now confirmed by his absence during four subsequent trappings.

At that, of 97 chicks banded during the decade, 65290 was the only one contriving to survive for five winters. Three reached 4 years, 7 reached 3 years, 19 reached 2 years, and 67 disappeared after their first winter. Hence if I were selling insurance to chicks, I could compute the premium with assurance. But this would raise the problem: in what currency would I pay the widows? I suppose in ants' eggs.

I know so little about birds that I can only speculate on why 65290 survived his fellows. Was he more clever in dodging his enemies? What enemies? A chickadee is almost too small to have any. That whimsical fellow called Evolution, having enlarged the dinosaur until he tripped over his own toes, tried shrinking the chickadee until he was just too big to be snapped up by flycatchers as an insect, and just too little to be pursued by hawks and owls as meat. Then he regarded his handiwork and laughed. Everyone laughs at so small a bundle of large enthusiasms.

The sparrow hawk, the screech owl, the shrike, and especially the midget saw-whet owl might find it worth while to kill a chickadee, but I've only once found evidence of actual murder: a screech-owl pellet contained one of my bands. Perhaps these small bandits have a fellow-feeling for midgets.

It seems likely that weather is the only killer so devoid of both humor and dimension as to kill a chickadee. I suspect that in the chickadee Sunday School two mortal sins are taught: thou shalt not venture into windy places in winter, thou shalt not get wet before a blizzard.

I learned the second commandment one drizzly winter dusk while watching a band of chicks going to roost in my woods. The drizzle came out of the south, but I could tell it would turn northwest and bitter cold before morning. The chicks went to bed in a dead oak, the bark of which had peeled and warped into curls, cups, and hollows of various sizes, shapes, and exposures. The bird selecting a roost dry against a south drizzle, but vulnerable to a north one, would surely be frozen by morning. The bird selecting a roost dry from all sides would awaken safe. This, I think, is the kind of wisdom that spells survival in chickdom, and accounts for 65290 and his like.

The chickadee's fear of windy places is easily deduced from his behavior. In winter he ventures away from woods only on calm days, and the distance varies inversely as the breeze. I know several wind-swept woodlots that are chickless all winter, but are freely used at all other seasons. They are wind-swept because cows have browsed out the undergrowth. To the steam-heated banker who mortgages the farmer who needs more cows who need more pasture, wind is a minor nuisance, except perhaps at the Flatiron corner. To the chickadee, winter wind is the boundary of the habitable world. If the chickadee had an office, the maxim over his desk would say: 'Keep calm.'

His behavior at the trap discloses the reason. Turn your trap so that he must enter with even a moderate wind at his tail, and all the king's horses cannot drag him to the bait. Turn it the other way, and your score may be good. Wind from behind blows cold and wet under the feathers, which are his portable roof and air-conditioner. Nuthatches, juncos, tree sparrows, and woodpeckers likewise fear winds from behind, but their heating plants and hence their wind tolerance are larger in the order named. Books on nature seldom mention wind; they are written behind stoves.

I suspect there is a third commandment in chickdom: thou shalt investigate every loud noise. When we start chopping in our woods, the chicks at once appear and stay until the felled tree or riven log has exposed new insect eggs or pupae for their delectation. The discharge of a gun will likewise summon chicks, but with less satisfactory dividends.

What served as their dinner bell before the day of

axes, mauls, and guns? Presumably the crash of falling trees. In December 1940, an ice-storm felled an extraordinary number of dead snags and living limbs in our woods. Our chicks scoffed at the trap for a month, being replete with the dividends of the storm.

65290 has long since gone to his reward. I hope that in his new woods, great oaks full of ants' eggs keep falling all day long, with never a wind to ruffle his composure or take the edge off his appetite. And I hope that he still wears my band.

Part II
The Quality of Landscape

Wisconsin

Marshland Elegy

A DAWN wind stirs on the great marsh. With almost imperceptible slowness it rolls a bank of fog across the wide morass. Like the white ghost of a glacier the mists advance, riding over phalanxes of tamarack, sliding across bogmeadows heavy with dew. A single silence hangs from horizon to horizon.

Out of some far recess of the sky a tinkling of little bells falls soft upon the listening land. Then again silence. Now comes a baying of some sweet-throated hound, soon the clamor of a responding pack. Then a far clear blast of hunting horns, out of the sky into the fog.

High horns, low horns, silence, and finally a pandemonium of trumpets, rattles, croaks, and cries that almost shakes the bog with its nearness, but without yet disclosing whence it comes. At last a glint of sun reveals the approach of a great echelon of birds. On motionless wing they emerge from the lifting mists, sweep a final arc of sky, and settle in clangorous descending spirals to their feeding grounds. A new day has begun on the crane marsh.

*   *   *

A sense of time lies thick and heavy on such a place. Yearly since the ice age it has awakened each spring to the clangor of cranes. The peat layers that comprise the bog are laid down in the basin of an ancient lake. The cranes stand, as it were, upon the sodden pages of their own history. These peats are the compressed remains of the mosses that clogged the pools, of the tamaracks that spread over the moss, of the cranes that bugled over the tamaracks since the retreat of the ice sheet. An endless caravan of generations has built of its own bones this bridge into the future, this habitat where the oncoming host again may live and breed and die.

To what end? Out on the bog a crane, gulping some luckless frog, springs his ungainly hulk into the air and flails the morning sun with mighty wings. The tamaracks re-echo with his bugled certitude. He seems to know.

*   *   *

Our ability to perceive quality in nature begins, as in art, with the pretty. It expands through successive stages of the beautiful to values as yet uncaptured by language. The quality of cranes lies, I think, in this higher gamut, as yet beyond the reach of words.

This much, though, can be said: our appreciation of the crane grows with the slow unraveling of earthly history. His tribe, we now know, stems out of the remote Eocene. The other members of the fauna in which he originated are long since entombed within the hills. When we hear his call we hear no mere bird. He is the symbol of our untamable past, of that incredible sweep of millennia which underlies and conditions the daily affairs of birds and men.

And so they live and have their being—these cranes —not in the constricted present, but in the wider reaches of evolutionary time. Their annual return is the ticking of the geologic clock. Upon the place of their return they confer a peculiar distinction. Amid the endless mediocrity of the commonplace, a crane marsh holds a paleontological patent of nobility, won in the march of aeons, and revocable only by shotgun. The sadness discernible in some marshes arises, perhaps, from their once having harbored cranes. Now they stand humbled, adrift in history.

Some sense of this quality in cranes seems to have been felt by sportsmen and ornithologists of all ages. Upon such quarry as this the Holy Roman Emperor Frederick loosed his gyrfalcons. Upon such quarry as this once swooped the hawks of Kublai Khan. Marco Polo tells us: 'He derives the highest amusement from sporting with gyrfalcons and hawks. At Changanor the Khan has a great Palace surrounded by a fine plain where are found cranes in great numbers. He causes millet and other grains to be sown in order that the birds may not want.'

The ornithologist Bengt Berg, seeing cranes as a boy upon the Swedish heaths, forthwith made them his life work. He followed them to Africa and discovered their winter retreat on the White Nile. He says of his first encounter: 'It was a spectacle which eclipsed the flight of the roc in the Thousand and One Nights.'

*   *   *

When the glacier came down out of the north, crunching hills and gouging valleys, some adventuring rampart of the ice climbed the Baraboo Hills and fell back into the outlet gorge of the Wisconsin River. The swollen waters backed up and formed a lake half as long as the state, bordered on the east by cliffs of ice, and fed by the torrents that fell from melting mountains. The shorelines of this old lake are still visible; its bottom is the bottom of the great marsh.

The lake rose through the centuries, finally spilling over east of the Baraboo range. There it cut a new channel for the river, and thus drained itself. To the residual lagoons came the cranes, bugling the defeat of the retreating winter, summoning the on-creeping host of living things to their collective task of marsh-building. Floating bogs of sphagnum moss clogged the lowered waters, filled them. Sedge and leather-leaf, tamarack and spruce successively advanced over the bog, anchoring it by their root fabric, sucking out its water, making peat. The lagoons disappeared, but not the cranes. To the moss-meadows that replaced the ancient waterways they returned each spring to dance and bugle and rear their gangling sorrel-colored young. These, albeit birds, are not properly called chicks, but *colts*. I cannot explain why. On some dewy June morning watch them gambol over their ancestral pastures at the heels of the roan mare, and you will see for yourself.

One year not long ago a French trapper in buckskins pushed his canoe up one of the moss-clogged creeks that thread the great marsh. At this attempt to invade their miry stronghold the cranes gave vent to loud and ribald laughter. A century or two later Englishmen came in covered wagons. They chopped clearings in the timbered moraines that border the marsh, and in them planted corn and buckwheat. They did not intend, like a Great Khan at Changanor, to feed the cranes. But the cranes do not question the intent of glaciers, emperors, or pioneers. They ate the grain, and when some irate farmer failed to concede their usufruct in his corn, they trumpeted a warning and sailed across the marsh to another farm.

There was no alfalfa in those days, and the hill-farms made poor hay land, especially in dry years. One dry year someone set a fire in the tamaracks. The burn grew up quickly to bluejoint grass, which, when cleared of dead trees, made a dependable hay meadow. After that, each August, men appeared to cut hay. In winter, after the cranes had gone South, they drove wagons over the frozen bogs and hauled the hay to their farms in the hills. Yearly they plied the marsh with fire and axe, and in two short decades hay meadows dotted the whole expanse.

Each August when the haymakers came to pitch their camps, singing and drinking and lashing their teams with whip and tongue, the cranes whinnied to their colts and retreated to the far fastnesses. 'Red shitepokes' the haymakers called them, from the rusty hue which at that season often stains the battleship-gray of crane plumage. After the hay was stacked and the marsh again their own, the cranes returned, to call down out of October skies the migrant flocks from Canada. Together they wheeled over the new-cut stubbles and raided the corn until frosts gave the signal for the winter exodus.

These haymeadow days were the Arcadian age for marsh dwellers. Man and beast, plant and soil lived on and with each other in mutual toleration, to the mutual benefit of all. The marsh might have kept on producing hay and prairie chickens, deer and musk-rat, crane-music and cranberries forever.

The new overlords did not understand this. They did not include soil, plants, or birds in their ideas of mutuality. The dividends of such a balanced econ-omy were too modest. They envisaged farms not only around, but *in* the marsh. An epidemic of ditch-digging and land-booming set in. The marsh was grid-ironed with drainage canals, speckled with new fields and farmsteads.

But crops were poor and beset by frosts, to which the expensive ditches added an aftermath of debt. Farmers moved out. Peat beds dried, shrank, caught fire. Sun-energy out of the Pleistocene shrouded the countryside in acrid smoke. No man raised his voice against the waste, only his nose against the smell. After a dry summer not even the winter snows could extinguish the smoldering marsh. Great pockmarks were burned into field and meadow, the scars reach-ing down to the sands of the old lake, peat-covered these hundred centuries. Rank weeds sprang out of the ashes, to be followed after a year or two by aspen scrub. The cranes were hard put, their numbers shrinking with the remnants of unburned meadow. For them, the song of the power shovel came near being an elegy. The high priests of progress knew nothing of cranes, and cared less. What is a species more or less among engineers? What good is an undrained marsh anyhow?

For a decade or two crops grew poorer, fires deeper, wood-fields larger, and cranes scarcer, year by year. Only reflooding, it appeared, could keep the peat from burning. Meanwhile cranberry growers had, by plugging drainage ditches, reflooded a few spots and obtained good yields. Distant politicians bugled about marginal land, over-production, unemployment relief, conservation. Economists and planners came to look at the marsh. Surveyors, technicians, CCC's, buzzed about. A counter-epidemic of reflooding set in. Government bought land, resettled farmers, plugged ditches wholesale. Slowly the bogs are re-wetting. The firepocks become ponds. Grass fires still burn, but they can no longer burn the wetted soil.

All this, once the CCC camps were gone, was good for cranes, but not so the thickets of scrub popple that spread inexorably over the burns, and still less the maze of new roads that inevitably follow governmental conservation. To build a road is so much simpler than to think of what the country really needs. A roadless marsh is seemingly as worthless to the alphabetical conservationist as an undrained one was to the empire-builders. Solitude, the one natural resource still undowered of alphabets, is so far recognized as valuable only by ornithologists and cranes.

Thus always does history, whether of marsh market place, end in paradox. The ultimate value in these marshes is wildness, and the crane is wildness incarnate. But all conservation of wildness is self-defeating, for to cherish we must see and fondle, and when enough have seen and fondled, there is no wilderness left to cherish.

*   *   *

Some day, perhaps in the very process of our benefactions, perhaps in the fullness of geologic time, the last crane will trumpet his farewell and spiral skyward from the great marsh. High out of the clouds will fall the sound of hunting horns, the baying of the phantom pack, the tinkle of little bells, and then a silence never to be broken, unless perchance in some far pasture of the Milky Way.

The Sand Counties

Every profession keeps a small herd of epithets, and needs a pasture where they may run at large. Thus economists must find free range somewhere for their pet aspersions, such as submarginality, regression, and institutional rigidity. Within the ample reaches of the Sand Counties these economic terms of reproach find beneficial exercise, free pasturage, and immunity from the gadflies of critical rebuttal.

Soil experts, likewise, would have a hard life without the Sand Counties. Where else would their podzols, gleys, and anaerobics find a living?

Social planners have, of late years, come to use the Sand Counties for a different, albeit somewhat parallel, purpose. The sandy region serves as a pale blank area, of pleasing shape and size, on those polka-dot maps where each dot represents ten bathtubs, or five women's auxiliaries, or one mile of black-top, or a share in a blooded bull. Such maps would become monotonous if stippled uniformly.

In short, the Sand Counties are poor.

Yet in the 1930's, when the alphabetical uplifts galloped like forty horsemen across the Big Flats, exhorting the sand farmers to resettle elsewhere, these benighted folk did not want to go, even when baited with 3 per cent at the federal land bank. I began to wonder why, and finally, to settle the question, I bought myself a sand farm.

Sometimes in June, when I see unearned dividends of dew hung on every lupine, I have doubts about the real poverty of the sands. On solvent farmlands lupines do not even grow, much less collect a daily rainbow of jewels. If they did, the weed-control officer, who seldom sees a dewy dawn, would doubtless insist that they be cut. Do economists know about lupines?

Perhaps the farmers who did not want to move out of the Sand Counties had some deep reason, rooted far back in history, for preferring to stay. I am reminded of this every April when the pasque-flowers bloom on every gravelly ridge. Pasques do not say much, but I infer that their preference harks back to the glacier that put the gravel there. Only gravel ridges are poor enough to offer pasques full elbow-room in April sun. They endure snows, sleets, and bitter winds for the privilege of blooming alone.

There are other plants who seem to ask of this world not riches but room. Such is the little sandwort that throws a white-lace cap over the poorest hill-tops just before the lupines splash them with blue.

Sandworts simply refuse to live on a good farm, even on a very good farm, complete with rock garden and begonias. And then there is the little Linaria, so small, so slender, and so blue that you don't even see it until it is directly underfoot; who ever saw a Linaria except on a sandblow?

Finally there is Draba, beside whom even Linaria is tall and ample. I have never met an economist who knows Draba, but if I were one I should do all my economic pondering lying prone on the sand, with Draba at nose-length.

There are birds that are found only in the Sand Counties, for reasons sometimes easy, sometimes diffi-cult, to guess. The clay-colored sparrow is there, for the clear reason that he is enamored of jackpines, and jackpines of sand. The sandhill crane is there, for the clear reason that he is enamored of solitude, and there is none left elsewhere. But why do wood-cocks prefer to nest in the sandy regions? Their pref-erence is rooted in no such mundane matter as food, for earthworms are far more abundant on better soils. After years of study, I now think I know the reason. The male woodcock, while doing his peenting prologue to the sky dance, is like a short lady in high heels: he does not show up to advantage in dense tangled ground cover. But on the poorest sand-streak of the poorest pasture or meadow of the Sand Coun-ties, there is, in April at least, no ground cover at all, save only moss, Draba, cardamine, sheep-sorrel, and Antennaria, all negligible impediments to a bird with short legs. Here the male woodcock can puff and strut and mince, not only without let or hindrance, but in full view of his audience, real or hoped-for. This little circumstance, important for only an hour a day, for only one month of the year, perhaps for only one of the two sexes, and certainly wholly irrelevant to economic standards of living, determines the woodcock's choice of a home.

The economists have not yet tried to resettle woodcocks.

Odyssey

X had marked time in the limestone ledge since the Paleozoic seas covered the land. Time, to an atom locked in a rock, does not pass.

The break came when a bur-oak root nosed down a crack and began prying and sucking. In the flash of a century the rock decayed, and X was pulled out and up into the world of living things. He helped build a flower, which became an acorn, which fattened a deer, which fed an Indian, all in a single year.

From his berth in the Indian's bones, X joined again in chase and flight, feast and famine, hope and fear. He felt these things as changes in the little chemical pushes and pulls that tug timelessly at every atom. When the Indian took his leave of the prairie, X moldered briefly underground, only to embark on a second trip through the bloodstream of the land.

This time it was a rootlet of bluestem that sucked him up and lodged him in a leaf that rode the green billows of the prairie June, sharing the common task of hoarding sunlight. To this leaf also fell an uncommon task: flicking shadows across a plover's eggs. The ecstatic plover, hovering overhead, poured praises on something perfect: perhaps the eggs, perhaps the shadows, or perhaps the haze of pink phlox that lay on the prairie.

When the departing plovers set wing for the Argentine, all the bluestems waved farewell with tall new tassels. When the first geese came out of the north and all the bluestems glowed wine-red, a forehanded deermouse cut the leaf in which X lay, and buried it in an underground nest, as if to hide a bit of Indian summer from the thieving frosts. But a fox detained the mouse, molds and fungi took the nest apart, and X lay in the soil again, foot-loose and fancy-free.

Next he entered a tuft of side-oats grama, a buffalo, a buffalo chip, and again the soil. Next a spiderwort, a rabbit, and an owl. Thence a tuft of sporobolus.

All routines come to an end. This one ended with a prairie fire, which reduced the prairie plants to smoke, gas, and ashes. Phosphorus and potash atoms stayed in the ash, but the nitrogen atoms were gone with the wind. A spectator might, at this point, have predicted an early end of the biotic drama, for with fires exhausting the nitrogen, the soil might well have lost its plants and blown away.

But the prairie had two strings to its bow. Fires thinned its grasses, but they thickened its stand of leguminous herbs: prairie clover, bush clover, wild bean, vetch, lead-plant, trefoil, and Baptisia, each carrying its own bacteria housed in nodules on its rootlets. Each nodule pumped nitrogen out of the air into the plant, and then ultimately into the soil.

Thus the prairie savings bank took in more nitrogen from its legumes than it paid out to its fires. That the prairie is rich is known to the humblest deer-mouse; why the prairie is rich is a question seldom asked in all the still lapse of ages.

Between each of his excursions through the biota, X lay in the soil and was carried by the rains, inch by inch, downhill. Living plants retarded the wash by impounding atoms; dead plants by locking them to their decayed tissues. Animals ate the plants and carried them briefly uphill or downhill, depending on whether they died or defecated higher or lower than they fed. No animal was aware that the altitude of his death was more important than his manner of dying. Thus a fox caught a gopher in a meadow, carrying X uphill to his bed on the brow of a ledge, where an eagle laid him low. The dying fox sensed the end of his chapter in foxdom, but not the new beginning in the odyssey of an atom.

An Indian eventually inherited the eagle's plumes, and with them propitiated the Fates, whom he assumed had a special interest in Indians. It did not occur to him that they might be busy casting dice against gravity; that mice and men, soils and songs, might be merely ways to retard the march of atoms to the sea.

One year, while X lay in a cottonwood by the river, he was eaten by a beaver, an animal that always feeds higher than he dies. The beaver starved when his pond dried up during a bitter frost. X rode the carcass down the spring freshet, losing more altitude each hour than heretofore in a century. He ended up in the silt of a backwater bayou, where he fed a crayfish, a coon, and then an Indian, who laid him down to his last sleep in a mound on the river-bank. One spring an oxbow caved the bank, and after one short week of freshet X lay again in his ancient prison, the sea.

An atom at large in the biota is too free to know freedom; an atom back in the sea has forgotten it. For every atom lost to the sea, the prairie pulls another out of the decaying rocks. The only certain truth is that its creatures must suck hard, live fast, and die often, lest its losses exceed its gains.

*   *   *

It is the nature of roots to nose into cracks. When Y was thus released from the parent ledge, a new animal had arrived and begun redding up the prairie to fit his own notions of law and order. An oxteam turned the prairie sod, and Y began a succession of dizzy annual trips through a new grass called wheat.

The old prairie lived by the diversity of its plants and animals, all of which were useful because the sum total of their co-operations and competitions achieved continuity. But the wheat farmer was a builder of categories; to him only wheat and oxen were useful. He saw the useless pigeons settle in clouds upon his wheat, and shortly cleared the skies of them. He saw the chinch bugs take over the stealing job, and fumed because here was a useless thing too small to kill. He failed to see the downward wash of over-wheated loam, laid bare in spring against the pelting rains. When soil-wash and chinch bugs finally put an end to wheat farming, Y and his like had already traveled far down the watershed.

When the empire of wheat collapsed, the settler took a leaf from the old prairie book: he impounded his fertility in livestock, he augmented it with nitrogen-pumping alfalfa, and he tapped the lower layers of the loam with deep-rooted corn.

But he used his alfalfa, and every other new weapon against wash, not only to hold his old plowings, but also to exploit new ones which, in turn, needed holding.

So, despite alfalfa, the black loam grew gradually thinner. Erosion engineers built dams and terraces to hold it. Army engineers built levees and wing-dams to flush it from the rivers. The rivers would not flush, but raised their beds instead, thus choking navigation. So the engineers built pools like gigantic beaver ponds, and Y landed in one of these, his trip from rock to river completed in one short century.

On first reaching the pool, Y made several trips through water plants, fish, and waterfowl. But engineers build sewers as well as dams, and down them comes the loot of all the far hills and the sea. The atoms that once grew pasque-flowers to greet the returning plovers now lie inert, confused, imprisoned in oily sludge.

Roots still nose among the rocks. Rains still pelt the fields. Deermice still hide their souvenirs of Indian summer. Old men who helped destroy the pigeons still recount the glory of the fluttering hosts. Black and white buffalo pass in and out of red barns, offering free rides to itinerant atoms.

On a Monument to the Pigeon[1]

We have erected a monument to commemorate the funeral of a species. It symbolizes our sorrow. We grieve because no living man will see again the on-rushing phalanx of victorious birds, sweeping a path for spring across the March skies, chasing the defeated winter from all the woods and prairies of Wisconsin.

Men still live who, in their youth, remember pigeons. Trees still live who, in their youth, were shaken by a living wind. But a decade hence only the oldest oaks will remember, and at long last only the hills will know.

There will always be pigeons in books and in museums, but these are effigies and images, dead to all hardships and to all delights. Book-pigeons cannot dive out of a cloud to make the deer run for cover, or clap their wings in thunderous applause of mast-laden woods. Book-pigeons cannot breakfast on new-mown wheat in Minnesota, and dine on blueberries in Canada. They know no urge of seasons; they feel no kiss of sun, no lash of wind and weather. They live forever by not living at all.

Our grandfathers were less well-housed, well-fed, well-clothed than we are. The strivings by which they bettered their lot are also those which deprived us of pigeons. Perhaps we now grieve because we are not sure, in our hearts, that we have gained by the exchange. The gadgets of industry bring us more comforts than the pigeons did, but do they add as much to the glory of the spring?

It is a century now since Darwin gave us the first

[1] The monument to the Passenger Pigeon, placed in Wyalusing State Park, Wisconsin, by the Wisconsin Society for Ornithology. Dedicated 11 May 1947.

glimpse of the origin of species. We know now what was unknown to all the preceding caravan of generations: that men are only fellow-voyagers with other creatures in the odyssey of evolution. This new knowledge should have given us, by this time, a sense of kinship with fellow-creatures; a wish to live and let live; a sense of wonder over the magnitude and duration of the biotic enterprise.

Above all we should, in the century since Darwin, have come to know that man, while now captain of the adventuring ship, is hardly the sole object of its quest, and that his prior assumptions to this effect arose from the simple necessity of whistling in the dark.

These things, I say, should have come to us. I fear they have not come to many.

For one species to mourn the death of another is a new thing under the sun. The Cro-Magnon who slew the last mammoth thought only of steaks. The sportsman who shot the last pigeon thought only of his prowess. The sailor who clubbed the last auk thought of nothing at all. But we, who have lost our pigeons, mourn the loss. Had the funeral been ours, the pigeons would hardly have mourned us. In this fact, rather than in Mr. DuPont's nylons or Mr. Vannevar Bush's bombs, lies objective evidence of our superiority over the beasts.

*   *   *

This monument, perched like a duckhawk on this cliff, will scan this wide valley, watching through the days and years. For many a March it will watch the geese go by, telling the river about clearer, colder, lonelier waters on the tundra. For many an April it will see the redbuds come and go, and for many a

May the flush of oak-blooms on a thousand hills. Questing wood ducks will search these basswoods for hollow limbs; golden prothonotaries will shake golden pollen from the river willows, Egrets will pose on these sloughs in August; plovers will whistle from September skies. Hickory nuts will plop into October leaves, and hail will rattle in November woods. But no pigeons will pass, for there are no pigeons, save only this flightless one, graven in bronze on this rock. Tourists will read this inscription, but their thoughts will not take wing.

We are told by economic moralists that to mourn the pigeon is mere nostalgia; that if the pigeoners had not done away with him, the farmers would ultimately have been obliged, in self-defense, to do so.

This is one of those peculiar truths that are valid, but not for the reasons alleged.

The pigeon was a biological storm. He was the lightning that played between two opposing potentials of intolerable intensity: the fat of the land and the oxygen of the air. Yearly the feathered tempest roared up, down, and across the continent, sucking up the laden fruits of forest and prairie, burning them in a traveling blast of life. Like any other chain reaction, the pigeon could survive no dimunution of his own furious intensity. When the pigeoners subtracted from his numbers, and the pioneers chopped gaps in the continuity of his fuel, his flame guttered out with hardly a sputter or even a wisp of smoke.

Today the oaks still flaunt their burden at the sky, but the feathered lightning is no more. Worm and weevil must now perform slowly and silently the biological task that once drew thunder from the firmament.

The wonder is not that the pigeon went out, but that he ever survived through all the millennia of pre-Babbittian time.

*   *   *

The pigeon loved his land: he lived by the intensity of his desire for clustered grape and bursting beechnut, and by his contempt of miles and seasons. Whatever Wisconsin did not offer him gratis today, he sought and found tomorrow in Michigan, or Labrador, or Tennessee. His love was for present things, and these things were present somewhere; to find them required only the free sky, and the will to ply his wings.

To love what *was* is a new thing under the sun, unknown to most people and to all pigeons. To see America as history, to conceive of destiny as a becoming, to smell a hickory tree through the still lapse of ages—all these things are possible for us, and to achieve them takes only the free sky, and the will to ply our wings. In these things, and not in Mr. Bush's bombs and Mr. DuPont's nylons, lies objective evidence of our superiority over the beasts.

Flambeau

People who have never canoed a wild river, or who have done so only with a guide in the stern, are apt to assume that novelty, plus healthful exercise, account for the value of the trip. I thought so too, until I met the two college boys on the Flambeau.

Supper dishes washed, we sat on the bank watching a buck dunking for water plants on the far shore. Soon the buck raised his head, cocked his ears upstream, and then bounded for cover.

Around the bend now came the cause of his alarm: two boys in a canoe. Spying us, they edged in to pass the time of day.

'What time is it?' was their first question. They explained that their watches had run down, and for the first time in their lives there was no clock, whistle, or radio to set watches by. For two days they had lived by 'sun-time,' and were getting a thrill out of it. No servant brought them meals: they got their meat out of the river, or went without. No traffic cop whistled them off the hidden rock in the next rapids. No friendly roof kept them dry when they misguessed whether or not to pitch the tent. No guide showed them which camping spots offered a nightlong breeze, and which a nightlong misery of mosquitoes; which firewood made clean coals, and which only smoke.

Before our young adventurers pushed off downstream, we learned that both were slated for the Army upon the conclusion of their trip. Now the *motif* was clear. This trip was their first and last taste of freedom, an interlude between two regimentations: the campus and the barracks. The elemental simplicities of wilderness travel were thrills not only because of their novelty, but because they represented complete freedom to make mistakes, The wilderness gave them their first taste of those rewards and penalties for wise and foolish acts which every woodsman faces daily, but against which civilization has built a thousand buffers. These boys were 'on their own' in this particular sense.

Perhaps every youth needs an occasional wilderness trip, in order to learn the meaning of this particular freedom.

When I was a small boy, my father used to describe

all choice camps, fishing waters, and woods as 'nearly as good as the Flambeau.' When I finally launched my own canoe in this legendary stream, I found it up to expectations as a river, but as a wilderness it was on its last legs. New cottages, resorts, and highway bridges were chopping up the wild stretches into shorter and shorter segments. To run down the Flambeau was to be mentally whipsawed between alternating impressions: no sooner had you built up the mental illusion of being in the wilds than you sighted a boat-landing, and soon you were coasting past some cottager's peonies.

Safely past the peonies, a buck bounding up the bank helped us to restore the wilderness flavor, and the next rapids finished the job. But staring at you beside the pool below was a synthetic log cabin, complete with composition roof, 'Bide-A-Wee' signboard, and rustic pergola for afternoon bridge.

Paul Bunyan was too busy a man to think about posterity, but if he had asked to reserve a spot for posterity to see what the old north woods looked like, he likely would have chosen the Flambeau, for here the cream of the white pine grew on the same acres with the cream of the sugar maple, yellow birch, and hemlock. This rich intermixture of pine and hardwoods was and is uncommon. The Flambeau pines, growing on a hardwood soil richer than pines are ordinarily able to occupy, were so large and valuable, and so close to a good log-driving stream, that they were cut at an early day, as evidenced by the decayed condition of their giant stumps. Only defective pines were spared, but there are enough of these alive today to punctuate the skyline of the

Flambeau with many a green monument to bygone days.

The hardwood logging came much later; in fact, the last big hardwood company 'pulled steel' on its last logging railroad only a decade ago. All that remains of that company today is a 'land-office' in its ghost town, selling off its cutovers to hopeful settlers. Thus died an epoch in American history: the epoch of cut out and get out.

Like a coyote rummaging in the offal of a deserted camp, the post-logging economy of the Flambeau subsists on the leavings of its own past. 'Gypo' pulpwood cutters nose around in the slashings for the occasional small hemlock overlooked in the main logging. A portable sawmill crew dredges the riverbed for sunken 'deadheads,' many of which drowned during the hell-for-leather log-drives of the glory days. Rows of these mud-stained corpses are drawn up on shore at the old landings—all in perfect condition, and some of great value, for no such pine exists in the north woods today. Post and pole cutters strip the swamps of white cedar; the deer follow them around and strip the felled tops of their foliage. Everybody and everything subsists on leavings.

So complete are all these scavengings that when the modern cottager builds a log cabin, he uses imitation logs sawed out of slab piles in Idaho or Oregon, and hauled to Wisconsin woods in a freight car. The proverbial coals to Newcastle seem a mild irony compared with this.

Yet there remains the river, in a few spots hardly changed since Paul Bunyan's day; at early dawn, before the motor boats awaken, one can still hear it singing in the wilderness. There are a few sections of uncut timber, luckily state-owned. And there is a considerable remnant of wildlife: muskellunge, bass, and sturgeon in the river; mergansers, black ducks, and wood ducks breeding in the sloughs; ospreys, eagles, and ravens cruising overhead. Everywhere are deer, perhaps too many: I counted 52 in two days afloat. A wolf or two still roams the upper Flambeau, and there is a trapper who claims he saw a marten, though no marten skin has come out of the Flambeau since 1900.

Using these remnants of the wilderness as a nucleus, the State Conservation Department began, in 1943, to rebuild a fifty-mile stretch of river as a wild area for the use and enjoyment of young Wisconsin. This wild stretch is set in a matrix of state forest, but there is to be no forestry on the river banks, and as few road crossings as possible. Slowly, patiently, and sometimes expensively the Conservation Department has been buying land, removing cottages, warding off unnecessary roads, and in general pushing the clock back, as far as possible, toward the original wilderness.

The good soil that enabled the Flambeau to grow the best cork pine for Paul Bunyan likewise enabled Rusk County, during recent decades, to sprout a dairy industry. These dairy farmers wanted cheaper electric power than that offered by local power companies, hence they organized a co-operative REA and in 1947 applied for a power dam, which, when built, would clip off the lower reaches of a fifty-mile stretch in process of restoration as canoe-water.

There was a sharp and bitter political fight. The Legislature, sensitive to farmer-pressure but oblivious of wilderness values, not only approved the REA dam, but deprived the Conservation Commission of any future voice in the disposition of power sites. It thus seems likely that the remaining canoe-water on the Flambeau, as well as every other stretch of wild river in the state, will ultimately be harnessed for power.

Perhaps our grandsons, having never seen a wild river, will never miss the chance to set a canoe in singing waters.

Deadening

The old oak had been girdled and was dead.

There are degrees of death in abandoned farms. Some old houses cock an eye at you as if to say 'Somebody will move in. Wait and see.'

But this farm was different. Girdling the old oak to squeeze one last crop out of the barnyard has the same finality as burning the furniture to keep warm.

Illinois and Iowa

Illinois Bus Ride

A FARMER and his son are out in the yard, pulling a crosscut saw through the innards of an ancient cottonwood. The tree is so large and so old that only a foot of blade is left to pull on.

Time was when that tree was a buoy in the prairie
sea. George Rogers Clark may have camped under it;
buffalo may have nooned in its shade, switching flies.
Every spring it roosted fluttering pigeons. It is the
best historical library short of the State College, but
once a year it sheds cotton on the farmer's window
screens. Of these two facts, only the second is
important.

The State College tells farmers that Chinese elms do
not clog screens, and hence are preferable to cottonwoods. It likewise pontificates on cherry preserves,
Bang's disease, hybrid corn, and beautifying the farm
home. The only thing it does not know about farms
is where they came from. Its job is to make Illinois
safe for soybeans.

I am sitting in a 60-mile-an-hour bus sailing over
a highway originally laid out for horse and buggy.
The ribbon of concrete has been widened and widened until the field fences threaten to topple into the
road cuts. In the narrow thread of sod between the
shaved banks and the toppling fences grow the relics
of what once was Illinois: the prairie.

No one in the bus sees these relics. A worried farmer,
his fertilizer bill projecting from his shirt pocket,
looks blankly at the lupines, lespedezas, or Baptisias
that originally pumped nitrogen out of the prairie
air and into his black loamy acres. He does not distinguish them from the parvenu quack-grass in which
they grow. Were I to ask him why his corn makes a
hundred bushels, while that of non-prairie states does
well to make thirty, he would probably answer that
Illinois soil is better. Were I to ask him the name of

that white spike of pea-like flowers hugging the fence, he would shake his head. A weed, likely.

A cemetery flashes by, its borders alight with prairie puccoons. There are no puccoons elsewhere; dog-fennels and sowthistles supply the yellow *motif* for the modern landscape. Puccoons converse only with the dead.

Through the open window I hear the heart-stirring whistle of an upland plover; time was when his fore-bears followed the buffalo as they trudged shoulder-deep through an illimitable garden of forgotten blooms. A boy spies the bird and remarks to his father: there goes a snipe.

*   *   *

The sign says, 'You are entering the Green River Soil Conservation District.' In smaller type is a list of who is co-operating; the letters are too small to be read from a moving bus. It must be a roster of who's who in conservation.

The sign is neatly painted. It stands in a creek-bottom pasture so short you could play golf on it. Near by is the graceful loop of an old dry creek bed. The new creek bed is ditched straight as a ruler; it has been 'uncurled' by the county engineer to hurry the run-off. On the hill in the background are con-toured strip-crops; they have been 'curled' by the ero-sion engineer to retard the run-off. The water must be confused by so much advice.

*   *   *

Everything on this farm spells money in the bank. The farmstead abounds in fresh paint, steel, and con-crete. A date on the barn commemorates the founding fathers. The roof bristles with lightning rods, the weathercock is proud with new gilt. Even the pigs look solvent.

The old oaks in the woodlot are without issue. There are no hedges, brush patches, fencerows, or other signs of shiftless husbandry. The cornfield has fat steers, but probably no quail. The fences stand on narrow ribbons of sod; whoever plowed that close to barbed wires must have been saying, 'Waste not, want not.'

In the creek-bottom pasture, flood trash is lodged high in the bushes. The creek banks are raw; chunks of Illinois have sloughed off and moved seaward. Patches of giant ragweed mark where freshets have thrown down the silt they could not carry. Just who is solvent? For how long?

* * *

The highway stretches like a taut tape across the corn, oats, and clover fields; the bus ticks off the opulent miles; the passengers talk and talk and talk. About what? About baseball, taxes, sons-in-law, movies, motors, and funerals, but never about the heaving groundswell of Illinois that washes the windows of the speeding bus. Illinois has no genesis, no history, no shoals or deeps, no tides of life and death. To them Illinois is only the sea on which they sail to ports unknown.

Red Legs Kicking

When I call to mind my earliest impressions, I wonder whether the process ordinarily referred to as grow-

ing up is not actually a process of growing down; whether experience, so much touted among adults as the thing children lack, is not actually a progressive dilution of the essentials by the trivialities of living. This much at least is sure: my earliest impressions of wildlife and its pursuit retain a vivid sharpness of form, color, and atmosphere that half a century of professional wildlife experience has failed to obliterate or to improve upon.

Like most aspiring hunters, I was given, at an early age, a single-barreled shotgun and permission to hunt rabbits. One winter Saturday, *en route* to my favorite rabbit patch, I noticed that the lake, then covered with ice and snow, had developed a small 'airhole' at a point where a windmill discharged warm water from the shore. All ducks had long since departed southward, but I then and there formulated my first ornithological hypothesis: if there were a duck left in the region, he (or she) would inevitably, sooner or later, drop in at this airhole. I suppressed my appetite for rabbits (then no mean feat), sat down in the cold smartweeds on the frozen mud, and waited.

I waited all afternoon, growing colder with each passing crow, and with each rheumatic groan of the laboring windmill. Finally, at sunset, a lone black duck came out of the west, and without even a preliminary circling of the airhole, set his wings and pitched downward.

I cannot remember the shot; I remember only my unspeakable delight when my first duck hit the snowy ice with a thud and lay there, belly up, red legs kicking.

When my father gave me the shotgun, he said I might hunt partridges with it, but that I might not shoot them from trees. I was old enough, he said, to learn wing-shooting.

My dog was good at treeing partridge, and to forego a sure shot in the tree in favor of a hopeless one at the fleeing bird was my first exercise in ethical codes. Compared with a treed partridge, the devil and his seven kingdoms was a mild temptation.

At the end of my second season of featherless partridge-hunting I was walking, one day, through an aspen thicket when a big partridge rose with a roar at my left, and, towering over the aspens, crossed behind me, hell-bent for the nearest cedar swamp. It was a swinging shot of the sort the partridge-hunter dreams about, and the bird tumbled dead in a shower of feathers and golden leaves.

I could draw a map today of each clump of red bunchberry and each blue aster that adorned the mossy spot where he lay, my first partridge on the wing. I suspect my present affection for bunchberries and asters dates from that moment.

Arizona and New Mexico

On Top

WHEN I first lived in Arizona, the White Mountain was a horseman's world. Except along a few main routes, it was too rough for wagons. There were no cars. It was too big for foot travel; even sheepherders rode. Thus by elimination, the county-sized plateau known as 'on top' was the exclusive domain of the mounted man: mounted cowman, mounted sheepman, mounted forest officer, mounted trapper, and those unclassified mounted men of unknown origin and uncertain destination always found on frontiers. It is difficult for this generation to understand this aristocracy of space based upon transport.

No such thing existed in the railroad towns two days to the north, where you had your choice of travel by shoe leather, burro, cowhorse, buckboard, freight wagon, caboose, or Pullman. Each of these modes of movement corresponded to a social caste, the members of which spoke a distinctive vernacular, wore distinctive clothes, ate distinctive food, and patronized different saloons, Their only common denominator was a democracy of debt to the general store, and a communal wealth of Arizona dust and Arizona sunshine.

As one proceeded southward across the plains and mesas toward the White Mountain, these castes dropped out one by one as their respective modes of travel became impossible, until finally, 'on top,' the horsemen ruled the world.

Henry Ford's revolution has of course abolished all this. Today the plane has given even the sky to Tom, Dick, and Harry.

*   *   *

In winter the top of the mountain was denied even to horsemen, for the snow piled deep on the high meadows, and the little canyons up which the only trails ascended drifted full to the brim. In May every canyon roared with an icy torrent, but soon thereafter you could 'top out'—if your horse had the heart to climb half a day through knee-deep mud.

In the little village at the foot of the mountain there existed, each spring, a tacit competition to be the first rider to invade the high solitudes. Many of

us tried it, for reasons we did not stop to analyze. Rumor ran fast. Whoever did it first wore a kind of horseman's halo. He was 'man-of-the-year.'

The mountain spring, storybooks to the contrary notwithstanding, did not come with a rush. Balmy days alternated with bitter winds, even after the sheep had gone up. I have seen few colder sights than a drab gray mountain meadow, sprinkled with complaining ewes and half-frozen lambs, pelted by hail and snow. Even the gay nutcrackers humped their backs to these spring storms.

The mountain in summer had as many moods as there were days and weathers; the dullest rider, as well as his horse, felt these moods to the marrow of his bones.

On a fair morning the mountain invited you to get down and roll in its new grass and flowers (your less inhibited horse did just this if you failed to keep a tight rein), Every living thing sang, chirped, and burgeoned. Massive pines and firs, storm-tossed these many months, soaked up the sun in towering dignity. Tassel-eared squirrels, poker-faced but exuding emotion with voice and tail, told you insistently what you already knew full well: that never had there been so rare a day, or so rich a solitude to spend it in.

An hour later, thunderheads may have blotted out the sun, while your erstwhile paradise cowered under the impending lash of lightning, rain, and hail. Black gloom hung poised, as over a bomb with the fuse lighted. Your horse jumped at every rolling pebble, every crackling twig. When you turned in the saddle to unlash your slicker, he shied, snorted, and trembled as if you were about to unfurl the scroll of an Apocalypse. When I hear anyone say he does not fear lightning, I still remark inwardly: he has never ridden The Mountain in July.

The explosions are fearsome enough, but more so are the smoking slivers of stone that sing past your ear when the bolt crashes into a rimrock. Still more so are the splinters that fly when a bolt explodes a pine. I remember one gleaming white one, 15 feet long, that stabbed deep into the earth at my feet and stood there humming like a tuning fork.

It must be poor life that achieves freedom from fear.

*   *   *

The top of the mountain was a great meadow, half a day's ride across, but do not picture it as a single amphitheater of grass, hedged in by a wall of pines. The edges of that meadow were scrolled, curled, and crenulated with an infinity of bays and coves, points and stringers, peninsulas and parks, each one of which differed from all the rest. No man knew them all, and every day's ride offered a gambler's chance of finding a new one. I say 'new' because one often had the feeling, riding into some flower-spangled cove, that if anyone had ever been here before, he must of necessity have sung a song, or written a poem.

This feeling of having this day discovered the incredible accounts, perhaps, for the profusion of initials, dates, and cattle brands inscribed on the patient bark of aspens at every mountain camp site. In these inscriptions one could, in any day, read the history of *Homo texanus* and his culture, not in the cold categories of anthropology, but in terms of the individual career of some founding father whose initials you recognized as the man whose son bested you at horse-trading, or whose daughter you once danced with. Here, dated in the 'nineties, was his simple initial, without brand, inscribed no doubt when he first arrived alone on the mountain as an itinerant cowpuncher. Next, a decade later, his initial plus brand; by that time he had become a solid citizen with an 'outfit,' acquired by thrift, natural increase, and perhaps a nimble rope. Next, only a few years old, you found his daughter's initial, inscribed by some enamored youth aspiring not only to the lady's hand, but to the economic succession.

The old man was dead now; in his later years his heart had thrilled only to his bank account and to the tally of his flocks and herds, but the aspen revealed that in his youth he too had felt the glory of the mountain spring.

The history of the mountain was written not only in aspen bark, but in its place names. Cow-country place names are lewd, humorous, ironic, or sentimental, but seldom trite. Usually they are subtle enough to draw inquiry from new arrivals, whereby hangs that web of tales which, full spun, constitutes the local folklore.

For example, there was 'The Boneyard,' a lovely meadow where bluebells arched over the half-buried skulls and scattered vertebrae of cows long since dead. Here in the 1880's a foolish cowman, newly arrived from the warm valleys of Texas, had trusted the allurements of the mountain summer and essayed to winter his herd on mountain hay. When the November storms hit, he and his horse had floundered out, but not his cows.

Again, there was 'The Campbell Blue,' a headwater of the Blue River to which an early cowman had brought himself a bride. The lady, tiring of rocks and trees, had yearned for a piano. A piano was duly fetched, a Campbell piano. There was only one mule in the county capable of packing it, and only one packer capable of the almost superhuman task' of balancing such a load. But the piano failed to bring contentment; the lady decamped; and when the story was told me, the ranch cabin was already a ruin of sagging logs.

Again there was 'Frijole Cienega,' a marshy meadow walled in by pines, under which stood, in my day, a small log cabin used by any passer-by as an overnight camp. It was the unwritten law for the owner of such real estate to leave flour, lard, and beans, and for the passer-by to replenish such stock as he could. But one luckless traveler, trapped there for a week by storms, had found only beans. This breach of hospitality was sufficiently notable to be handed down to history as a place name.

Finally, there was 'Paradise Ranch,' an obvious platitude when read from a map, but something quite different when you arrived there at the end of a hard ride. It lay tucked away on the far side of a high peak, as any proper paradise should. Through its verdant meadows meandered a singing trout stream. A horse left for a month on this meadow waxed so fat that rain-water gathered in a pool on his back. After my first visit to Paradise Ranch I remarked to myself: what else *could* you call it?

*   *   *

Despite several opportunities to do so, I have never returned to the White Mountain. I prefer not to see what tourists, roads, sawmills, and logging railroads have done for it, or to it. I hear young people, not yet born when I first rode out 'on top,' exclaim about it as a wonderful place. To this, with an unspoken mental reservation, I agree.

Thinking Like a Mountain

A deep chesty bawl echoes from rimrock to rimrock, rolls down the mountain, and fades into the far blackness of the night. It is an outburst of wild defiant sorrow, and of contempt for all the adversities of the world.

Every living thing (and perhaps many a dead one as well) pays heed to that call. To the deer it is a reminder of the way of all flesh, to the pine a forecast of midnight scuffles and of blood upon the snow, to the coyote a promise of gleanings to come, to the cowman a threat of red ink at the bank, to the hunter a challenge of fang against bullet. Yet behind these obvious and immediate hopes and fears there lies a deeper meaning, known only to the mountain itself. Only the mountain has lived long enough to listen objectively to the howl of a wolf.

Those unable to decipher the hidden meaning know nevertheless that it is there, for it is felt in all wolf country, and distinguishes that country from all other land. It tingles in the spine of all who hear wolves by night, or who scan their tracks by day. Even without sight or sound of wolf, it is implicit in a hundred small events: the midnight whinny of a pack horse, the rattle of rolling rocks, the bound of a fleeing deer, the way shadows lie under the spruces. Only the in-educable tyro can fail to sense the presence or absence of wolves, or the fact that mountains have a secret opinion about them.

My own conviction on this score dates from the day I saw a wolf die. We were eating lunch on a high rimrock, at the foot of which a turbulent river elbowed its way. We saw what we thought was a doe fording the torrent, her breast awash in white water. When she climbed the bank toward us and shook out her tail, we realized our error: it was a wolf. A half-dozen others, evidently grown pups, sprang from the willows and all joined in a welcoming mêlée of wagging tails and playful maulings. What was literally a pile of wolves writhed and tumbled in the center of an open flat at the foot of our rimrock.

In those days we had never heard of passing up a chance to kill a wolf. In a second we were pumping lead into the pack, but with more excitement than accuracy: how to aim a steep downhill shot is always confusing. When our rifles were empty, the old wolf was down, and a pup was dragging a leg into im-passable slide-rocks.

We reached the old wolf in time to watch a fierce green fire dying in her eyes. I realized then, and have known ever since, that there was something new to me in those eyes—something known only to her and to the mountain. I was young then, and full of trigger-itch; I thought that because fewer wolves meant more deer, that no wolves would mean hunters' paradise. But after seeing the green fire die, I sensed that neither the wolf nor the mountain agreed with such a view.

*　　　*　　　*

Since then I have lived to see state after state extirpate its wolves. I have watched the face of many a newly wolfless mountain, and seen the south-facing slopes wrinkle with a maze of new deer trails. I have seen every edible bush and seedling browsed, first to anaemic desuetude, and then to death. I have seen every edible tree defoliated to the height of a saddle-

horn. Such a mountain looks as if someone had given God a new pruning shears, and forbidden Him all other exercise. In the end the starved bones of the hoped-for deer herd, dead of its own too-much, bleach with the bones of the dead sage, or molder under the high-lined junipers.

I now suspect that just as a deer herd lives in mortal fear of its wolves, so does a mountain live in mortal fear of its deer. And perhaps with better cause, for while a buck pulled down by wolves can be replaced in two or three years, a range pulled down by too many deer may fail of replacement in as many decades.

So also with cows. The cowman who cleans his range of wolves does not realize that he is taking over the wolf's job of trimming the herd to fit the range. He has not learned to think like a mountain. Hence we have dustbowls, and rivers washing the future into the sea.

*   *   *

We all strive for safety, prosperity, comfort, long life, and dullness. The deer strives with his supple legs, the cowman with trap and poison, the statesman with pen, the most of us with machines, votes, and dollars, but it all comes to the same thing: peace in our time. A measure of success in this is all well enough, and perhaps is a requisite to objective thinking, but too much safety seems to yield only danger in the long run. Perhaps this is behind Thoreau's dictum: In wildness is the salvation of the world. Perhaps this is the hidden meaning in the howl of the wolf, long known among mountains, but seldom perceived among men.

Escudilla

Life in Arizona was bounded under foot by grama grass, overhead by sky, and on the horizon by Escudilla.

To the north of the mountain you rode on honey-colored plains. Look up anywhere, any time, and you saw Escudilla.

To the east you rode over a confusion of wooded mesas. Each hollow seemed its own small world, soaked in sun, fragrant with juniper, and cozy with the chatter of piñon jays. But top out on a ridge and you at once became a speck in an immensity. On its edge hung Escudilla.

To the south lay the tangled canyons of Blue River, full of whitetails, wild turkeys, and wilder cattle. When you missed a saucy buck waving his goodbye over the skyline, and looked down your sights to wonder why, you looked at a far blue mountain: Escudilla.

To the west billowed the outliers of the Apache National Forest. We cruised timber there, converting the tall pines, forty by forty, into notebook figures representing hypothetical lumber piles. Panting up a canyon, the cruiser felt a curious incongruity between the remoteness of his notebook symbols and the immediacy of sweaty fingers, locust thorns, deer-fly bites, and scolding squirrels. But on the next ridge a cold wind, roaring across a green sea of pines, blew his doubts away. On the far shore hung Escudilla.

The mountain bounded not only our work and our play, but even our attempts to get a good dinner. On winter evenings we often tried to ambush a mallard on the river flats. The wary flocks circled the rosy west, the steel-blue north, and then disappeared into the inky black of Escudilla. If they reappeared on set wings, we had a fat drake for the Dutch oven. If they failed to reappear, it was bacon and beans again.

There was, in fact, only one place from which you did not see Escudilla on the skyline: that was the top of Escudilla itself. Up there you could not see the mountain, but you could feel it. The reason was the big bear.

Old Bigfoot was a robber-baron, and Escudilla was his castle. Each spring, when the warm winds had softened the shadows on the snow, the old grizzly crawled out of his hibernation den in the rock slides and, descending the mountain, bashed in the head of a cow. Eating his fill, he climbed back to his crags, and there summered peaceably on marmots, conies, berries, and roots.

I once saw one of his kills. The cow's skull and neck were pulp, as if she had collided head-on with a fast freight.

No one ever saw the old bear, but in the muddy springs about the base of the cliffs you saw his incredible tracks. Seeing them made the most hard-bitten cowboys aware of bear. Wherever they rode they saw the mountain, and when they saw the mountain they thought of bear. Campfire conversation ran to beef, *bailes*, and bear. Bigfoot claimed for his own only a cow a year, and a few square miles of useless rocks, but his personality pervaded the county.

Those were the days when progress first came to the cow country. Progress had various emissaries.

One was the first transcontinental automobilist. The cowboys understood this breaker of roads; he talked the same breezy bravado as any breaker of bronchos.

They did not understand, but they listened to and looked at, the pretty lady in black velvet who came to enlighten them, in a Boston accent, about woman suffrage.

They marveled, too, at the telephone engineer who strung wires on the junipers and brought instantaneous messages from town. An old man asked whether the wire could bring him a side of bacon.

One spring, progress sent still another emissary, a government trapper, a sort of St. George in overalls, seeking dragons to slay at government expense. Were there, he asked, any destructive animals in need of slaying? Yes, there was the big bear.

The trapper packed his mule and headed for Escudilla.

In a month he was back, his mule staggering under a heavy hide. There was only one barn in town big enough to dry it on. He had tried traps, poison, and all his usual wiles to no avail. Then he had erected a set-gun in a defile through which only the bear could pass, and waited. The last grizzly walked into the string and shot himself.

It was June. The pelt was foul, patchy, and worthless. It seemed to us rather an insult to deny the last grizzly the chance to leave a good pelt as a memorial to his race. All he left was a skull in the National Museum, and a quarrel among scientists over the Latin name of the skull.

It was only after we pondered on these things that we began to wonder who wrote the rules for progress.

* * *

Since the beginning, time had gnawed at the basaltic hulk of Escudilla, wasting, waiting, and building. Time built three things on the old mountain, a venerable aspect, a community of minor animals and plants, and a grizzly.

The government trapper who took the grizzly knew he had made Escudilla safe for cows. He did not know he had toppled the spire off an edifice a-building since the morning stars sang together.

The bureau chief who sent the trapper was a biologist versed in the architecture of evolution, but he did not know that spires might be as important as cows. He did not foresee that within two decades

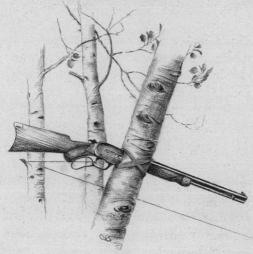

the cow country would become tourist country, and as such have greater need of bears than of beefsteaks.

The Congressmen who voted money to clear the ranges of bears were the sons of pioneers. They acclaimed the superior virtues of the frontiersman, but they strove with might and main to make an end of the frontier.

We forest officers, who acquiesced in the extinguishment of the bear, knew a local rancher who had plowed up a dagger engraved with the name of one one of Coronado's captains. We spoke harshly of the Spaniards who, in their zeal for gold and converts, had needlessly extinguished the native Indians. It did not occur to us that we, too, were the captains of an invasion too sure of its own righteousness.

Escudilla still hangs on the horizon, but when you see it you no longer think of bear. It's only a mountain now.

Chihuahua and Sonora

Guacamaja

THE PHYSICS of beauty is one department of natural science still in the Dark Ages. Not even the manipulators of bent space have tried to solve its equations. Everybody knows, for example, that the autumn landscape in the north woods is the land, plus a red maple, plus a ruffed grouse. In terms of conventional physics, the grouse represents only a millionth of either the mass or the energy of an acre. Yet subtract the grouse and the whole thing is dead. An enormous amount of some kind of motive power has been lost.

It is easy to say that the loss is all in our mind's eye, but is there any sober ecologist who will agree? He knows full well that there has been an ecological death, the significance of which is inexpressible in terms of contemporary science. A philosopher has called this imponderable essence the *numenon* of material things. It stands in contradistinction to *phenomenon*, which is ponderable and predictable, even to the tossings and turnings of the remotest star.

The grouse is the numenon of the north woods, the blue jay of the hickory groves, the whisky-jack

of the muskegs, the piñonero of the juniper foothills.
Ornithological texts do not record these facts. I suppose they are new to science, however obvious to the
discerning scientist. Be that as it may, I here record
the discovery of the numenon of the Sierra Madre:
the Thick-billed Parrot.

He is a discovery only because so few have visited
his haunts. Once there, only the deaf and blind could
fail to perceive his role in the mountain life and landscape. Indeed you have hardly finished breakfast before the chattering flocks leave their roost on the rimrocks and perform a sort of morning drill in the high
reaches of the dawn. Like squadrons of cranes they
wheel and spiral, loudly debating with each other
the question (which also puzzles you) whether this
new day which creeps slowly over the canyons is
bluer and golder than its predecessors, or less so. The
vote being a draw, they repair by separate companies
to the high mesas for their breakfast of pine-seed-
on-the-half-shell. They have not yet seen you.

But a little later, as you begin the steep ascent out
of the canyon, some sharp-eyed parrot, perhaps a
mile away, espies this strange creature puffing up the
trail where only deer or lion, bear or turkey, is
licensed to travel. Breakfast is forgotten. With a
whoop and a shout the whole gang is a-wing and
coming at you. As they circle overhead you wish fer-
vently for a parrot dictionary. Are they demanding
what-the-devil business have you in these parts? Or
are they, like an avian chamber-of-commerce, merely
making sure you appreciate the glories of their home
town, its weather, its citizens, and its glorious future

as compared with any and all other times and places whatsoever? It might be either or both. And there flashes through your mind the sad premonition of what will happen when the road is built, and this riotous reception committee first greets the tourist-with-a-gun.

It is soon clear that you are a dull inarticulate fellow, unable to respond by so much as a whistle to the standard amenities of the Sierra morn. And after all, there are more pine cones in the woods than have yet been opened, so let's finish breakfast! This time they may settle upon some tree below the rimrock, giving you the chance to sneak out to the edge and look down. There for the first time you see color: velvet green uniforms with scarlet and yellow epaulets and black helmets, sweeping noisily from pine to pine, but always in formation and always in even numbers. Only once did I see a gang of five, or any other number not comprised of pairs.

I do not know whether the nesting pairs are as noisy as these roistering flocks that greeted me in September. I do know that in September, if there are parrots on the mountain, you will soon know it. As a proper ornithologist, I should doubtless try to describe the call. It superficially resembles that of the piñon jay, but the music of the piñoneros is as soft and nostalgic as the haze hanging in their native canyons, while that of the Guacamaja is louder and full of the salty enthusiasm of high comedy.

In spring, I am told, the pair hunts up a woodpecker hole in some tall dead pine and performs its racial duty in temporary isolation. But what wood-

pecker excavates a hole large enough? The Guacamaja (as the natives euphoniously call the parrot) is
as big as a pigeon, and hardly to be squeezed into a
flicker-loft. Does he, with his own powerful beak,
perform the necessary enlargement? Or is he depen-
dent on the holes of the imperial woodpecker, which
is said to occur in these parts? To some future
ornithological visitor I bequeath the pleasant task of
discovering the answer.

The Green Lagoons

It is the part of wisdom never to revisit a wilderness, for the more golden the lily, the more certain that someone has gilded it. To return not only spoils a trip, but tarnishes a memory. It is only in the mind that shining adventure remains forever bright. For this reason, I have never gone back to the Delta of the Colorado since my brother and I explored it, by canoe, in 1922.

For all we could tell, the Delta had lain forgotten since Hernando de Alarcón landed there in 1540. When we camped on the estuary which is said to have harbored his ships, we had not for weeks seen a man or a cow, an axe-cut or a fence. Once we crossed an old wagon track, its maker unknown and its errand probably sinister. Once we found a tin can; it was pounced upon as a valuable utensil.

Dawn on the Delta was whistled in by Gambel quail, which roosted in the mesquites overhanging camp. When the sun peeped over the Sierra Madre, it slanted across a hundred miles of lovely desolation, a vast flat bowl of wilderness rimmed by jagged peaks. On the map the Delta was bisected by the river, but in fact the river was nowhere and everywhere, for he could not decide which of a hundred green lagoons offered the most pleasant and least speedy path to the Gulf. So he traveled them all, and so did we. He divided and rejoined, he twisted and turned, he meandered in awesome jungles, he all but ran in circles, he dallied with lovely groves, he got lost and was glad of it, and so were we. For the last word in procrastination, go travel with a river reluctant to lose his freedom in the sea.

'He leadeth me by still waters' was to us only a phrase in a book until we had nosed our canoe through the green lagoons. If David had not written the psalm, we should have felt constrained to write our own. The still waters were of a deep emerald hue, colored by algae, I suppose, but no less green for all that. A verdant wall of mesquite and willow separated the channel from the thorny desert beyond. At each bend we saw egrets standing in the pools ahead, each white statue matched by its white reflection. Fleets of cormorants drove their black prows in quest of skittering mullets; avocets, willets, and yellow-legs dozed one-legged on the bars; mallards, widgeons, and teal sprang skyward in alarm. As the birds took the air, they accumulated in a small cloud ahead, there to settle, or to break back to our rear. When a troop of egrets settled on a far green willow, they looked like a premature snowstorm.

All this wealth of fowl and fish was not for our delectation alone. Often we came upon a bobcat, flattened to some half-immersed driftwood log, paw poised for mullet. Families of raccoons waded the shallows, munching water beetles. Coyotes watched us from inland knolls, waiting to resume their breakfast of mesquite beans, varied, I suppose, by an occasional crippled shore bird, duck, or quail. At every shallow ford were tracks of burro deer. We always examined these deer trails, hoping to find signs of the despot of the Delta, the great jaguar, *el tigre*.

We saw neither hide nor hair of him, but his personality pervaded the wilderness; no living beast for-

got his potential presence, for the price of unwariness was death. No deer rounded a bush, or stopped to nibble pods under a mesquite tree, without a premonitory sniff for *el tigre*. No campfire died without talk of him. No dog curled up for the night, save at his master's feet; he needed no telling that the king of cats still ruled the night; that those massive paws could fell an ox, those jaws shear off bones like a guillotine.

By this time the Delta has probably been made safe for cows, and forever dull for adventuring hunters. Freedom from fear has arrived, but a glory has departed from the green lagoons.

When Kipling smelled the supper smokes of Amritsar, he should have elaborated, for no other poet has sung, or smelled, this green earth's firewoods. Most poets must have subsisted on anthracite.

On the Delta one burns only mesquite, the ultimate in fragrant fuels. Brittle with a hundred frosts and floods, baked by a thousand suns, the gnarled imperishable bones of these ancient trees lie ready-to-hand at every camp, ready to slant blue smoke across the twilight, sing a song of teapots, bake a loaf, brown a kettle of quail, and warm the shins of man and beast. When you have ladled a shovelful of mesquite coals under the Dutch oven, take care not to sit down in that spot before bedtime, lest you rise with a yelp that scares the quail roosting overhead. Mesquite coals have seven lives.

We had cooked with white-oak coals in the corn belt, we had smudged our pots with pine in the north woods, we had browned venison ribs over Arizona juniper, but we had not seen perfection until we roasted a young goose with Delta mesquite.

Those geese deserved the best of brownings, for they had bested us for a week. Every morning we watched the cackling phalanx head inland from the Gulf, shortly to return, replete and silent. What rare provender in what green lagoon was the object of their quest? Again and again we moved camp gooseward, hoping to see them settle, to find their banquet board. One day at about 8 a.m. we saw the phalanx circle, break ranks, sideslip, and fall to earth like maple leaves. Flock after flock followed. At long last we had found their rendezvous.

Next morning at the same hour we lay in wait beside an ordinary-looking slough, its bars covered with yesterday's goosetracks. We were already hungry, for it had been a long tramp from camp. My brother was eating a cold roast quail. The quail was halfway to his mouth when a cackle from the sky froze us to immobility. That quail hung in midair while the flock circled at leisure, debated, hesitated, and finally came in. That quail fell in the sand when the guns spoke, and all the geese we could eat lay kicking on the bar.

More came, and settled. The dog lay trembling. We ate quail at leisure, peering through the blind, listening to the small-talk. Those geese were gobbling *gravel*. As one flock filled up and left, another arrived, eager for their delectable stones. Of all the millions of pebbles in the green lagoons, those on this particular bar suited them best. The difference, to a snow goose, was worth forty miles of flying. It was worth a long hike to us.

Most small game on the Delta was too abundant to hunt. At every camp we hung up, in a few minutes' shooting, enough quail for tomorrow's use. Good gastronomy demanded at least one frosty night on the stringer as the necessary interlude between roosting in a mesquite and roasting over mesquite.

All game was of incredible fatness. Every deer laid down so much tallow that the dimple along his backbone would have held a small pail of water, had he allowed us to pour it. He didn't.

The origin of all this opulence was not far to seek. Every mesquite and every tornillo was loaded with pods. The dried-up mud flats bore an annual grass, the grain-like seeds of which could be scooped up by the cupful. There were great patches of a legume resembling coffeeweed; if you walked through these, your pockets filled up with shelled beans.

I remember one patch of wild melons, or *cala-basillas*, covering several acres of mudflat. The deer and coons had opened the frozen fruits, exposing the seeds. Doves and quail fluttered over this banquet like fruit-flies over a ripe banana.

We could not, or at least did not, eat what the quail and deer did, but we shared their evident delight in this milk-and-honey wilderness. Their festival mood became our mood; we all reveled in a common abundance and in each other's well-being. I cannot recall feeling, in settled country, a like sensitivity to the mood of the land.

Camp-keeping in the Delta was not all beer and skittles. The problem was water. The lagoons were saline; the river, where we could find it, was too muddy to drink. At each new camp we dug a new well. Most wells, however, yielded only brine from the Gulf. We learned, the hard way, where to dig for sweet water. When in doubt about a new well, we lowered the dog by his hind legs. If he drank freely, it was the signal for us to beach the canoe, kindle the fire, and pitch the tent. Then we sat at peace with the world while the quail sizzled in the Dutch oven, and the sun sank in glory behind the San Pedro Mártir. Later, dishes washed, we rehearsed the day, and listened to the noises of the night.

Never did we plan the morrow, for we had learned that in the wilderness some new and irresistible distraction is sure to turn up each day before breakfast. Like the river, we were free to wander.

To travel by plan in the Delta is no light matter; we were reminded of this whenever we climbed a cottonwood for a wider view. The view was so wide as to discourage prolonged scrutiny, especially toward the northwest, where a white streak at the foot of the Sierra hung in perpetual mirage. This was the great salt desert, on which, in 1829, Alexander Pattie died of thirst, exhaustion, and mosquitoes. Pattie had a plan: to cross the Delta to California.

Once we had a plan to portage from one green lagoon to a greener one. We knew it was there by the waterfowl hovering over it. The distance was 300 yards through a jungle of *cachinilla*, a tall spear-like shrub which grows in thickets of incredible density. The floods had bent down the spears, which opposed our passage in the manner of a Macedonian phalanx. We discreetly withdrew, persuaded that our lagoon was prettier anyhow.

Getting caught in a maze of *cachinilla* phalanxes was a real danger that no one had mentioned, whereas the danger we had been warned against failed to materialize. When we launched our canoe above the border, there were dire predictions of sudden death. Far huskier craft, we were told, had been overwhelmed by the tidal bore, a wall of water that rages up the river from the Gulf with certain incoming tides. We talked about the bore, we spun elaborate schemes to circumvent it, we even saw it in our dreams, with dolphins riding its crest and an aerial escort of screaming gulls. When we reached the mouth of the river, we hung our canoe in a tree and waited two days, but the bore let us down. It did not come.

The Delta having no place names, we had to devise our own as we went. One lagoon we called the Rillito, and it is here that we saw pearls in the sky. We were lying flat on our backs, soaking up November sun, staring idly at a soaring buzzard overhead. Far beyond him the sky suddenly exhibited a rotating circle of white spots, alternately visible and invisible. A faint bugle note soon told us they were cranes, inspecting their Delta and finding it good. At the time my ornithology was homemade, and I was pleased to think them whooping cranes because they were so white. Doubtless they were sandhill cranes, but it doesn't matter. What matters is that we were sharing our wilderness with the wildest of living fowl. We and they had found a common home in the remote fastnesses of space and time; we were both back in the Pleistocene. Had we been able to, we would have bugled back their greeting. Now, from the far reaches of the years, I see them wheeling still.

*　　*　　*

All this was far away and long ago. I am told the green lagoons now raise cantaloupes. If so, they should not lack flavor.

Man always kills the thing he loves, and so we the pioneers have killed our wilderness. Some say we had to. Be that as it may, I am glad I shall never be young without wild country to be young in. Of what avail are forty freedoms without a blank spot on the map?

Song of the Gavilan

The song of a river ordinarily means the tune that waters play on rock, root, and rapid.

The Rio Gavilan has such a song. It is a pleasant music, bespeaking dancing riffles and fat rainbows laired under mossy roots of sycamore, oak, and pine. It is also useful, for the tinkle of waters so fills the narrow canyon that deer and turkey, coming down out of the hills to drink, hear no footfall of man or horse. Look sharp as you round the next bend, for it may yield you a shot, and thus save a heart-breaking climb in the high mesas.

This song of the waters is audible to every ear, but there is other music in these hills, by no means audible to all. To hear even a few notes of it you must first live here for a long time, and you must know the speech of hills and rivers. Then on a still night, when the campfire is low and the Pleiades have climbed over rimrocks, sit quietly and listen for a wolf to howl, and think hard of everything you have seen and tried to understand. Then you may hear it—a vast pulsing harmony—its score inscribed on a thousand hills, its notes the lives and deaths of plants and animals, its rhythms spanning the seconds and the centuries.

The life of every river sings its own song, but in

most the song is long since marred by the discords of
misuse. Overgrazing first mars the plants and then the
soil. Rifle, trap, and poison next deplete the larger
birds and mammals; then comes a park or forest with
roads and tourists. Parks are made to bring the music
to the many, but by the time many are attuned to
hear it there is little left but noise.

There once were men capable of inhabiting a river
without disrupting the harmony of its life. They must
have lived in thousands on the Gavilan, for their
works are everywhere. Ascend any draw debouching
on any canyon and you find yourself climbing little
rock terraces or check dams, the crest of one level
with the base of the next. Behind each dam is a little
plot of soil that was once a field or garden, sub-
irrigated by the showers which fell on the steep
adjoining slopes. On the crest of the ridge you may
find the stone foundations of a watch tower; here the
hillside farmer probably stood guard over his polka-
dot acrelets. Household water he must have carried
from the river. Of domestic animals he evidently had
none. What crops did he raise? How long ago? The
only fragment of an answer lies in the 300-year-old
pines, oaks, or junipers that now find rootage in his
little fields. Evidently it was longer ago than the age
of the oldest trees.

The deer love to lie on these little terraces. They
afford a level bed, free of rocks, upholstered with
oak leaves, and curtained by shrubs. One bound over
the dam and the deer is out of sight of an intruder.

One day, by aid of a roaring wind, I crept down
upon a buck bedded on a dam. He lay in the shade
of a great oak whose roots grasped the ancient mas-

onary. His horns and ears were silhouetted against the golden grama beyond, in which grew the green rosette of a mescal. The whole scene had the balance of a well-laid centerpiece. I overshot, my arrow splintering on the rocks the old Indian had laid. As the buck bounded down the mountain with a goodbye wave of his snowy flag, I realized that he and I were actors in an allegory. Dust to dust, stone age to stone age, but always the eternal chase! It was appropriate that I missed, for when a great oak grows in what is now my garden, I hope there will be bucks to bed in its fallen leaves, and hunters to stalk, and miss, and wonder who built the garden wall.

Some day my buck will get a .30-.30 in his glossy ribs. A clumsy steer will appropriate his bed under the oak, and will munch the golden grama until it is replaced by weeds. Then a freshet will tear out the old dam, and pile its rocks against a tourist road along the river below. Trucks will churn the dust of the old trail on which I saw wolf tracks yesterday.

To the superficial eye the Gavilan is a hard and stony land, full of cruel slopes and cliffs, its trees too gnarled for post of sawlog, its ranges too steep for pasturage. But the old terrace-builders were not deceived; they knew it by experience to be a land of milk and honey. These twisted oaks and junipers bear each year a crop of mast to be had by wildlings for the pawing. The deer, turkeys, and javelinas spend their days, like steers in a cornfield, converting this mast into succulent meat. These golden grasses conceal, under their waving plumes, a subterranean garden of bulbs and tubers, including wild potatoes. Open the crop of a fat little Mearns' quail and you find an herbarium of subsurface foods scratched from the rocky ground you thought barren. These foods are the motive power which plants pump through that great organ called the fauna.

Every region has a human food symbolic of its fatness. The hills of the Gavilan find their gastronomic epitome in this wise: Kill a mast-fed buck, not earlier than November, not later than January. Hang him in a live-oak tree for seven frosts and seven suns. Then cut out the half-frozen 'straps' from their bed of tallow under the saddle, and slice them transversely into steaks. Rub each steak with salt, pepper, and flour. Throw into a Dutch oven containing deep smoking-hot bear fat and standing on live-oak coals. Fish out the steaks at the first sign of browning. Throw a little flour into the fat, then ice-cold water, then milk. Lay a steak on the summit of a steaming sour-dough biscuit and drown both in gravy.

This structure is symbolic. The buck lies on his mountain, and the golden gravy is the sunshine that floods his days, even unto the end.

Food is the continuum in the Song of the Gavilan. I mean, of course, not only your food, but food for the oak which feeds the buck who feeds the cougar who dies under an oak and goes back into acorns for his erstwhile prey. This is one of many food cycles starting from and returning to oaks, for the oak also feeds the jay who feeds the goshawk who named your river, the bear whose grease made your gravy, the quail who taught you a lesson in botany, and the turkey who daily gives you the slip. And the common end of all is to help the headwater trickles of the Favilan split one more grain of soil off the broad hulk of the Sierra Madre to make another oak.

There are men charged with the duty of examining the construction of the plants, animals, and soils which are the instruments of the great orchestra. These men are called professors. Each selects one instrument and spends his life taking it apart and describing its strings and sounding boards. This process of dismemberment is called research. The place for dismemberment is called a university.

A professor may pluck the strings of his own instrument, but never that of another, and if he listens for music he must never admit it to his fellows or to his students. For all are restrained by an ironbound taboo which decrees that the construction of instruments is the domain of science, while the detection of harmony is the domain of poets.

Professors serve science and science serves progress. It serves progress so well that many of the more intricate instruments are stepped upon and broken in the rush to spread progress to all backward lands. One by one the parts are thus stricken from the songs of songs. If the professor is able to classify each instrument before it is broken, he is well content.

Science contributes moral as well as material blessings to the world. Its great moral contribution is objectivity, or the scientific point of view. This means doubting everything except facts; it means hewing to the facts, let the chips fall where they may. One of the facts hewn to by science is that every river needs more people, and all people need more inventions, and hence more science; the good life depends on the indefinite extension of this chain of logic. That the good life on any river may likewise depend on the perception of its music, and the preservation of some music to perceive, is a form of doubt not yet entertained by science.

Science has not yet arrived on the Gavilan, so the otter plays tag in its pools and riffles and chases the fat rainbows from under its mossy banks with never a thought for the flood that one day will scour the bank into the Pacific, or for the sportsman who will one day dispute his title to the trout. Like the scientist, he has no doubts about his own design for living. He assumes that for him the Gavilan will sing forever.

Oregon and Utah

Cheat Takes Over

JUST AS there is honor among thieves, so there is solidarity and co-operation among plant and animal pests. Where one pest is stopped by natural barriers, another arrives to breach the same wall by a new approach. In the end every region and every resource get their quota of uninvited ecological guests.

Thus the English sparrow, rendered innocuous by the shrinkage in horses, was succeeded by the starling, who thrives in the wake of tractors. The chestnut blight, which had no passport beyond the west boundary of chestnuts, is being followed by the Dutch elm disease, with every chance of spreading to the west boundary of elms. The white-pine blister rust, stopped in its westward march by the treeless plains, effected a new landing via the back door, and is now romping down the Rockies from Idaho toward California.

Ecological stowaways began to arrive with the earliest settlements. The Swedish botanist, Peter Kalm, found most of the European weeds established in New Jersey and New York as early as 1750. They spread as rapidly as the settler's plow could prepare a suitable seedbed.

Others arrived later, from the West, and found

thousands of square miles of ready-made seedbed prepared by the trampling hoofs of range livestock. In such cases the spread was often so rapid as to escape recording; one simply woke up one fine spring to find the range dominated by a new weed. A notable instance was the invasion of the intermountain and northwestern foothills by downy chess or cheat grass (*Bromus tectorum*).

Lest you gain too optimistic an impression of this new ingredient of the melting pot, let me say that cheat is not a grass in the sense of forming a live sod. It is an annual weed of the grass family, like foxtail or crabgrass, dying each fall and reseeding that fall or the next spring. In Europe its habitat is the decaying straw of thatched roofs. The Latin word for roof is *tectum*, hence the label 'Brome of the roofs.' A plant that can make a living on the roof of a house can also thrive on this rich but arid roof of the continent.

Today the honey-colored hills that flank the northwestern mountains derive their hue not from the rich and useful bunchgrass and wheatgrass which once covered them, but from the inferior cheat which has replaced these native grasses. The motorist who exclaims about the flowing contours that lead his eye upward to far summits is unaware of this substitution. It does not occur to him that hills, too, cover ruined complexions with ecological face powder.

The cause of the substitution is overgrazing. When the too-great herds and flocks chewed and trampled the hide off the foothills, something had to cover the raw eroding earth. Cheat did.

Cheat grows in dense stands, and each stem bears a

mass of prickly awns which render the mature plant inedible to stock. To appreciate the predicament of a cow trying to eat mature cheat, try walking through it in low shoes. All field workers in cheat country wear high boots. Nylons are here relegated to running boards and concrete sidewalks.

These prickly awns cover the autumn hills with a yellow blanket as inflammable as cotton-wool. It is impossible fully to protect cheat country from fire. As a consequence, the remnants of good browse plants, such as sagebrush and bitterbrush, are being burned back to higher altitudes, where they are less useful as winter forage. The lower fringes of pine timber, needed as winter cover for deer and birds, are likewise being singed back to higher levels.

To a summer tourist, the burning of a few bushes off the foothills may seem a minor loss. He is unaware that, in winter, snow excludes both livestock and game from the higher mountains. Livestock can be fed on valley ranches, but deer and elk must find food in the foothills or starve. The habitable wintering belt is narrow, and the further north one goes, the greater is the disparity between the area of habitable winter range and the area of summer range. Hence these scattering foothill clumps of bitterbrush, sage, and oak, now fast shrinking under the onslaught of cheat fires, are the key to wildlife survival in the whole region. Besides, these scattered bushes often harbor, under their mechanical protection, remnants of native perennial grasses. When the bushes are burned off, these grass remnants succumb to livestock. While the sportsmen and stockmen wrangle over who should move first in easing the burden on the winter range, cheat grass is leaving less and less winter range to wrangle about.

Cheat gives rise to many minor irritations, most of them less important, perhaps, than starving deer or cheat-sores in a cow's mouth, but still worth mentioning. Cheat invades old alfalfa fields and degrades the hay. It blockades newly hatched ducklings from making the vital trek from upland nest to lowland water. It invades the lower fringe of lumber areas, where it chokes out seedling pines and threatens older reproduction with the danger of quick fire.

I experienced a minor irritation myself when I arrived at a 'port of entry' on the northern California border, where my car and baggage were searched by a quarantine officer. He explained politely that California welcomes tourists, but that she must make sure their baggage harbors no plant or animal pests. I asked him what pests. He recited a long list of prospective garden and orchard afflictions, but he did not mention the yellow blanket of cheat, which already extended from his feet to the far hills in every direction.

As is true of the carp, the starling, and the Russian thistle, the cheat-afflicted regions make a virtue of necessity and find the invader useful. Newly sprouted cheat is good forage while it lasts; like as not the lamb chop you ate for lunch was nurtured on cheat during the tender days of spring. Cheat reduces the erosion that would otherwise follow the overgrazing that admitted cheat. (This ecological ring-around-the-rosy merits long thought.)

I listened carefully for clues whether the West has accepted cheat as a necessary evil, to be lived with until kingdom come, or whether it regards cheat as a challenge to rectify its past errors in land-use. I found the hopeless attitude almost universal. There is, as yet, no sense of pride in the husbandry of wild plants and animals, no sense of shame in the proprietorship of a sick landscape. We tilt windmills in behalf of conservation in convention halls and editorial offices, but on the back forty we disclaim even owning a lance.

Manitoba

Clandeboye

EDUCATION, I fear, is learning to see one thing by going blind to another.

One thing most of us have gone blind to is the quality of marshes. I am reminded of this when, as a special favor, I take a visitor to Clandeboye, only to find that, to him, it is merely lonelier to look upon, and stickier to navigate, than other boggy places.

This is strange, for any pelican, duckhawk, godwit, or western grebe is aware that Clandeboye is a marsh apart. Why else do they seek it out in preference to other marshes? Why else do they resent my intrusion within its precincts not as mere trespass, but as some kind of cosmic impropriety?

I think the secret is this: Clandeboye is a marsh

apart, not only in space, but in time. Only the un-critical consumers of hand-me-down history suppose that 1941 arrived simultaneously in all marshes. The birds know better. Let a squadron of southbound pelicans but feel a lift of prairie breeze over Clande-boye, and they sense at once that here is a landing in the geological past, a refuge from that most relentless of aggressors, the future. With queer antediluvian grunts they set wing, descending in majestic spirals to the welcoming wastes of a bygone age.

Other refugees are already there, each accepting in his own fashion his respite from the march of time. Forster's terns, like troops of happy children, scream over the mud-flats as if the first cold melt from the retreating ice sheet were shivering the spines of their minnowy prey. A file of sandhill cranes bugles defiance of whatever it is that cranes distrust and fear. A flotilla of swans rides the bay in quiet dignity, bemoaning the evanescence of swanly things. From the tip of a storm-wracked cottonwood, where the marsh discharges into the big lake, a peregrine stoops playfully at passing fowl. He is gorged with duck meat, but it amuses him to terrorize the squealing teals. This, too, was his after-dinner sport in the days when Lake Agassiz covered the prairies.

It is easy to classify the attitudes of these wildlings, for each wears his heart on his sleeve. But there is one refugee in Clandeboye whose mind I cannot read, for he tolerates no truck with human intruders. Let other birds spill easy confidence to upstarts in over-alls, but not the western grebe! Stalk carefully as I will to the bordering reeds, all I get to see is a flash of silver as he sinks, soundless, into the bay. And then, from behind the reedy curtain of the far shore, he tinkles a little bell, warning all his kind of something. Of what?

I've never been able to guess, for there is some barrier between this bird and all mankind. One of my guests dismissed the grebe by checking off his name in the bird list, and jotting down a syllabic paraphrase of the tinkling bell: 'crick-crick,' or some such inanity. The man failed to sense that here was something more than a bird-call, that here was a *secret* message, calling not for rendition in counterfeit syllables, but for translation and understanding. Alas, I was, and still am, as helpless to translate it or to understand it as he.

As the spring advances, the bell grows persistent; at dawn and at dusk it tinkles from every open water. I infer that the young grebes are now launched in their watery career, and are receiving parental instruction in the grebe philosophy. But to *see* this schoolroom scene, that is not so easy.

One day I buried myself, prone, in the muck of a muskrat house. While my clothes absorbed local color, my eyes absorbed the lore of the marsh. A hen redhead cruised by with her convoy of ducklings, pink-billed fluffs of greenish-golden down. A Virginia rail nearly brushed my nose. The shadow of a pelican sailed over a pool in which a yellow-leg alighted with warbling whistle; it occurred to me that whereas I *write* a poem by dint of mighty cerebration, the yellow-leg *walks* a better one just by lifting his foot.

A mink slithered up the shore behind me, nose in air, trailing. Marsh wrens made trip after trip to a knot in the bulrushes, whence came the clamor of nestlings. I was starting to doze in the sun when there emerged from the open pool a wild red eye, glaring from the head of a bird. Finding all quiet, the silver body emerged: big as a goose, with the lines of a slim torpedo. Before I was aware of when or whence, a second grebe was there, and on her broad back rode two pearly-silver young, neatly enclosed in a corral of humped-up wings. All rounded a bend before I recovered my breath. And now I heard the bell, clear and derisive, behind the curtain of the reeds.

A sense of history should be the most precious gift of science and of the arts, but I suspect that the grebe, who has neither, knows more history than we do. His dim primordial brain knows nothing of who won the Battle of Hastings, but it seems to sense who won the battle of time. If the race of men were as old as the race of grebes, we might better grasp the import of his call. Think what traditions, prides, disdains, and wisdoms even a few self-conscious generations bring to us! What pride of continuity, then, impels this bird, who was a grebe eons before there was a man.

Be that as it may, the call of the grebe is, by some peculiar authority, the sound that dominates and unifies the marsh-land chorus. Perhaps, by some immemorial authority, he wields the baton for the whole biota. Who beats the measure for the lakeshore rollers as they build reef after reef for marsh after marsh, as age after age the waters recede to lower levels? Who holds sago and bulrush to their task of sucking sun and air, lest in winter the muskrats starve, and the canes engulf the marsh in lifeless jungle? Who counsels patience to brooding ducks by day, and incites bloodthirst in marauding minks by night? Who exhorts precision for the heron's spear, and speed for the falcon's fist? We assume, because all these creatures perform their diverse tasks without admonition audible to us, that they receive none, that their skills are inborn and their industry automatic, that weariness is unknown to the wild. Perhaps weariness is unknown only to grebes; perhaps it is the grebe who reminds them that if all are to survive, each must ceaselessly feed and fight, breed and die.

The marshlands that once sprawled over the prairie from the Illinois to the Athabasca are shrinking northward. Man cannot live by marsh alone, therefore he must needs live marshless. Progress cannot abide that farmland and marshland, wild and tame, exist in mutual toleration and harmony.

So with dredge and dyke, tile and torch, we sucked the cornbelt dry, and now the wheatbelt. Blue lake becomes green bog, green bog becomes caked mud, caked mud becomes a wheatfield.

Some day my marsh, dyked and pumped, will lie

forgotten under the wheat, just as today and yesterday will lie forgotten under the years. Before the last mud-minnow makes his last wiggle in the last pool, the terns will scream goodbye to Clandeboye, the swans will circle skyward in snowy dignity, and the cranes will blow their trumpets in farewell.

Part III
A Taste for Country

Country

THERE IS much confusion between land and country. Land is the place where corn, gullies, and mortgages grow. Country is the personality of land, the collective harmony of its soil, life, and weather. Country knows no mortgages, no alphabetical agencies, no tobacco road; it is calmly aloof to these petty exigencies of its alleged owners. That the previous occupant of my farm was a bootlegger mattered not one whit to its grouse; they sailed as proudly over the thickets as if they were guests of a king.

Poor land may be rich country, and vice versa. Only economists mistake physical opulence for riches. Country may be rich despite a conspicuous poverty of physical endowment, and its quality may not be apparent at first glance, nor at all times.

I know, for example, a certain lakeshore, a cool austerity of pines and wave-washed sands. All day you see it only as something for the surf to pound, a dark ribbon that stretches farther than you can paddle, a monotony to mark the miles by. But toward sunset some vagrant breeze may waft a gull across a headland, behind which a sudden roistering of loons reveals the presence of a hidden bay. You are seized with an impulse to land, to set foot on bearberry carpets, to pluck a balsam bed, to pilfer beach plums or blueberries, or perhaps to poach a partridge from out those bosky quietudes that lie behind the dunes. A bay? Why not also a trout stream? Incisively the paddles clip little soughing swirls athwart the gunwale, the bow swings sharp shoreward and cleaves the greening depths for camp.

Later, a supper-smoke hangs lazily upon the bay; a fire flickers under drooping boughs. It is a lean poor land, but rich country.

Some woods, perennially lush, are notably lacking in charm. Tall clean-boled oaks and tulip poplars may be good to look at, from the road, but once inside one may find a coarseness of minor vegetation, a turbidity of waters, and a paucity of wildlife. I cannot explain why a red rivulet is not a brook. Neither can I, by logical deduction, prove that a thicket without the potential roar of a quail covey is only a thorny place. Yet every outdoorsman knows that this is true. That wildlife is merely something to shoot at or to look at is the grossest of fallacies. It often represents the difference between rich country and mere land.

There are woods that are plain to look at, but not to look into. Nothing is plainer than a cornbelt woodlot; yet, if it be August, a crushed pennyroyal, or an

over-ripe mayapple, tells you here is a place. October sun on a hickory nut is irrefutable evidence of good country; one senses not only hickory but a whole chain of further sequences: perhaps of oak coals in the dusk, a young squirrel browning, and a distant barred owl hilarious over his own joke.

The taste for country displays the same diversity in aesthetic competence among individuals as the taste for opera, or oils. There are those who are willing to be herded in droves through 'scenic' places; who find mountains grand if they be proper moun-

tains with waterfalls, cliffs, and lakes. To such the
Kansas plains are tedious. They see the endless corn,
but not the heave and the grunt of ox teams breaking the prairie. History, for them, grows on campuses. They look at the low horizon, but they cannot
see it, as de Vaca did, under the bellies of the buffalo.

In country, as in people, a plain exterior often con-
ceals hidden riches, to perceive which requires much
living in and with. Nothing is more monotonous
than the juniper foothills, until some veteran of a
thousand summers, laden blue with berries, explodes
in a blue burst of chattering jays. The drab sogginess
of a March cornfield, saluted by one honker from
the sky, is drab no more.

A Man's Leisure Time

THE TEXT of this sermon is taken from the gospel according to Ariosto. I do not know the chapter and verse, but this is what he says: 'How miserable are the idle hours of the ignorant man!'

There are not many texts that I am able to accept as gospel truths, but this is one of them. I am willing to rise up and declare my belief that this text is literally true; true forward, true backward, true even before breakfast. The man who cannot enjoy his leisure is ignorant, though his degrees exhaust the alphabet, and the man who does enjoy his leisure is to some extent educated, though he has never seen the inside of a school.

I cannot easily imagine a greater fallacy than for one who has several hobbies to speak on the subject to those who may have none. For this implies prescription of avocation by one person for another, which is the antithesis of whatever virtue may inhere in having any at all. You do not annex a hobby, the hobby annexes you. To prescribe a hobby would be dangerously akin to prescribing a wife—with about the same probability of a happy outcome.

Let it be understood, then, that this is merely an exchange of reflections among those already obsessed—for better or for worse—with the need of doing something queer. Let others listen if they will, and profit by our behavior if they can.

What is a hobby anyway? Where is the line of demarcation between hobbies and ordinary normal pursuits? I have been unable to answer this question to my own satisfaction. At first blush I am tempted to conclude that a satisfactory hobby must be in large degree useless, inefficient, laborious, or irrelevant. Certainly many of our most satisfying avocations today consist of making something by hand which machines can usually make more quickly and cheaply, and sometimes better. Nevertheless I must in fairness admit that in a different age the mere fashioning of a machine might have been an excellent hobby. Galileo, I fancy, derived a real and personal satisfaction when he set the ecclesiastical world on its ear by embodying in a new catapult some natural law that St. Peter had inadvertently omitted to catalogue. Today the invention of a new machine, however noteworthy to industry, would, as a hobby, be trite stuff. Perhaps we have here the real inwardness of our question: A hobby is a defiance of the contemporary. It is an assertion of those permanent values which the momentary eddies of social evolution have contravened or overlooked. If this is true, then we may also say that every hobbyist is inherently a radical, and that his tribe is inherently a minority.

This, however, is serious; becoming serious is a grievous fault in hobbyists. It is an axiom that no hobby should either seek or need rational justification. To wish to do it is reason enough. To find reasons why it is useful or beneficial converts it at once from an avocation into an industry—lowers it at once to the ignominious category of an 'exercise' undertaken for health, power, or profit. Lifting dumbbells is not a hobby. It is a confession of subservience, not an assertion of liberty.

When I was a boy, there was an old German merchant who lived in a little cottage in our town. On Sundays he used to go out and knock chips off the limestone ledges along the Mississippi, and he had a great tonnage of these chips, all labeled and catalogued. The chips contained little fossil stems of some defunct water creatures called crinoids. The townspeople regarded this gentle old fellow as just a little bit abnormal, but harmless. One day the newspaper reported the arrival of certain titled strangers. It was whispered that these visitors were great scientists. Some of them were from foreign lands, and some among the world's leading paleontologists. They came to visit the harmless old man and to hear his pronouncements on crinoids, and they accepted these pronouncements as law. When the old German died, the town awoke to the fact that he was a world authority on his subject, a creator of knowledge, a maker of scientific history. He was a great man—a man beside whom the local captains of industry were mere bushwhackers. His collection went to a national museum, and his name is known in all the nations of the earth.

I knew a bank president who adventured in roses. Roses made him a happy man and a better bank president. I know a wheel manufacturer who adventures in tomatoes. He knows all about them, and, whether as a result or as a cause, he also knows all about wheels. I know a taxi driver who romances in sweet corn. Get him wound up once and you will be surprised how much he knows, and hardly less at how much there is to be known.

The most glamorous hobby I know of today is the revival of falconry. It has a few addicts in America, and perhaps a dozen in England—a minority indeed. For two and a half cents one can buy and shoot a cartridge that will kill the heron whose capture by hawking requires months or years of laborious training of both the hawk and the hawker. The cartridge, as a lethal agent, is a perfect product of industrial chemistry. One can write a formula for its lethal reaction. The hawk, as a lethal agent, is the perfect flower of that still utterly mysterious alchemy— evolution. No living man can, or possibly ever will, understand the instinct of predation that we share with our raptorial servant. No man-made machine can, or ever will, synthesize that perfect co-ordination of eye, muscle, and pinion as he stoops to his kill. The heron, if bagged, is inedible and hence useless (although the old falconers seem to have eaten him, just as a Boy Scout smokes and eats a flea-bitten summer cottontail that has fallen victim to his sling, club, or bow). Moreover the hawk, at the slightest error in technique of handling, may either 'go tame' like *Homo sapiens* or fly away into the blue. All in all, falconry is the perfect hobby.

To make and shoot the longbow is another. There is a subversive belief among laymen that in the hands of an expert the bow is an efficient weapon. Each fall, less than a hundred Wisconsin experts register to hunt deer with the broadheaded arrow. One out of

the hundred may get a buck, and he is surprised.
One out of five riflemen gets his buck. As an archer,
therefore, and on the basis of our record, I indignantly
deny the allegation of efficiency. I admit only this:
that making archery tackle is an effective alibi for

being late at the office, or failing to carry out the ashcan on Thursdays.

One cannot make a gun—at least I can't. But I can make a bow, and some of them will shoot. And this reminds me that perhaps our definition ought to be amended. A good hobby, in these times, is one that entails either making something or making the

tools to make it with, and then using it to accomplish some needless thing. When we have passed out of the present age, a good hobby will be the reverse of all these. I come again to the defiance of the contemporary.

A good hobby must also be a gamble. When I look at a rough, heavy, lumpy, splintery stave of *bois d'arc*, and envision the perfect gleaming weapon that will one day emerge from its graceless innards, and when I picture that bow, drawn in a perfect arc, ready—in a split second—to cleave the sky with its shining javelin, I must envision also the probability that it may—in a split second—burst into impotent splinters, while I face another laborious month of evenings at the bench. The possible debacle is, in short, an essential element in all hobbies, and stands in bold contradistinction to the humdrum certainty that the endless belt will eventuate in a Ford.

A good hobby may be a solitary revolt against the common-place, or it may be the joint conspiracy of a congenial group. That group may, on occasion, be the family. In either event it is a rebellion, and if a hopeless one, all the better. I cannot imagine a worse jumble than to have the whole body politic suddenly 'adopt' all the foolish ideas that smolder in happy discontent beneath the conventional surface of society. There is no such danger. Nonconformity is the highest evolutionary attainment of social animals, and will grow no faster than other new functions. Science is just beginning to discover what incredible regimentation prevails among the 'free' savages and the freer mammals and birds. A hobby is perhaps creation's first denial of the 'peck-order' that burdens the gregarious universe, and of which the majority of mankind is still a part.

The Round River

ONE OF the marvels of early Wisconsin was the Round River, a river that flowed into itself, and thus sped around and around in a never-ending circuit. Paul Bunyan discovered it, and the Bunyan saga tells how he floated many a log down its restless waters.

No one has suspected Paul of speaking in parables, yet in this instance he did. Wisconsin not only *had* a round river, Wisconsin *is* one. The current is the stream of energy which flows out of the soil into plants, thence into animals, thence back into the soil in a never ending circuit of life. 'Dust unto dust' is a desiccated version of the Round River concept.

We of the genus *Homo* ride the logs that float down the Round River, and by a little judicious 'burling' we have learned to guide their direction and speed. This feat entitles us to the specific appellation *sapiens*. The technique of burling is called economics, the remembering of old routes is called history, the selection of new ones is called statesmanship, the conversation about oncoming riffles and rapids is called politics. Some of the crew aspire to burl not only their own logs, but the whole flotilla as well. This collective bargaining with nature is called national planning.

In our educational system, the biotic continuum is seldom pictured to us as a stream. From our tenderest years we are fed with facts about the soils, floras, and faunas that comprise the channel of Round River (biology), about their origins in time (geology and evolution), about the technique of exploiting them (agriculture and engineering). But the concept of a current with drouths and freshets, backwaters and bars, is left to inference. To learn the hydrology of the biotic stream we must think at right angles to evolution and examine the collective behavior of biotic materials. This calls for a reversal of specialization; instead of learning more and more about less and less, we must learn more and more about the whole biotic landscape.

Ecology is a science that attempts this feat of thinking in a plane perpendicular to Darwin. Ecology is an infant just learning to talk, and, like other infants, is engrossed with its own coinage of big words. Its working days lie in the future. Ecology is destined to become the lore of Round River, a belated attempt to convert our collective knowledge of biotic materials into a collective wisdom of biotic navigation. This, in the last analysis, is conservation.

Conservation is a state of harmony between men and land. By land is meant all of the things on, over, or in the earth. Harmony with land is like harmony with a friend; you cannot cherish his right hand and chop off his left. That is to say, you cannot love game and hate predators; you cannot conserve the waters and waste the ranges; you cannot build the forest and mine the farm. The land is one organism. Its parts, like our own parts, compete with each other and co-operate with each other. The competitions are as much a part of the inner workings as the co-operations. You can regulate them—cautiously —but not abolish them.

The outstanding scientific discovery of the twentieth century is not television, or radio, but rather the complexity of the land organism. Only those who know the most about it can appreciate how little is known about it. The last word in ignorance is the man who says of an animal or plant: 'What good is it?' If the land mechanism as a whole is good, then every part is good, whether we understand it or not. If the biota, in the course of aeons, has built something we like but do not understand, then who but a fool would discard seemingly useless parts? To keep every cog and wheel is the first precaution of intelligent tinkering.

Have we learned this first principle of conservation: to preserve all the parts of the land mechanism? No, because even the scientist does not yet recognize all of them.

In Germany there is a mountain called the Spessart. Its south slope bears the most magnificent oaks in the world. American cabinetmakers, when they want the last word in quality, use Spessart oak. The north slope, which should be the better, bears an

indifferent stand of Scotch pine. Why? Both slopes
are part of the same state forest; both have been
managed with equally scrupulous care for two centuries. Why the difference?

Kick up the litter under the oak and you will see
that the leaves rot almost as fast as they fall. Under
the pines, though, the needles pile up as a thick
duff; decay is much slower. Why? Because in the
Middle Ages the south slope was preserved as a deer
forest by a hunting bishop; the north slope was pastured, plowed, and cut by settlers, just as we do with
our woodlots in Wisconsin and Iowa today. Only
after this period of abuse was the north slope re-
planted to pines. During this period of abuse something happened to the microscopic flora and fauna of
the soil. The number of species was greatly reduced,
i.e., the digestive apparatus of the soil lost some of
its parts. Two centuries of conservation have not
sufficed to restore these losses. It required the modern
microscope, and a century of research in soil science,
to discover the existence of these 'small cogs and
wheels' which determine harmony or disharmony
between men and land in the Spessart.

For the biotic community to survive, its internal
processes must balance, else its member-species would
disappear. That particular communities *do* survive for
long periods is well known: Wisconsin, for example,
in 1840 had substantially the same soil, fauna, and
flora as at the end of the ice age, i.e. 12,000 years
ago. We know this because the bones of its animals
and the pollens of its plants are preserved in the

peat bogs. The successive strata of peats, with their differing abundance of pollens, even record the weather; thus around 3000 B.C. an abundance of ragweed pollen indicates either a series of drouths, or a great stamping of buffalo, or severe fires on the prairie. These recurring exigencies did not prevent the survival of the 350 kinds of birds, 90 mammals, 150 fishes, 70 reptiles, or the thousands of insects and plants. That all these should survive as an internally balanced community for so many centuries shows an astonishing stability in the original biota. Science cannot explain the mechanisms of stability, but even a layman can see two of its effects: (1) Fertility, when extracted from rocks, circulated through such elaborate food chains that it accumulated as fast as or faster than it washed away. (2) This geological accumulation of soil fertility parallelled the diversification of flora and fauna; stability and diversity were apparently interdependent.

American conservation is, I fear, still concerned for the most part with show pieces. We have not yet learned to think in terms of small cogs and wheels. Look at our own back yard: at the prairies of Iowa and southern Wisconsin. What is the most valuable part of the prairie? The fat black soil, the chernozem. Who built the chernozem? The black prairie was built by the prairie plants, a hundred distinctive species of grasses, herbs, and shrubs; by the prairie fungi, insects, and bacteria; by the prairie mammals and birds, all interlocked in one humming community of co-operations and competitions, one biota. This biota, through ten thousand years of living and dying, burning and growing, preying and fleeing, freezing and thawing, built that dark and bloody ground we call prairie.

Our grandfathers did not, could not, know the origin of their prairie empire. They killed off the prairie fauna and they drove the flora to a last refuge on railroad embankments and roadsides. To our engineers this flora is merely weeds and brush; they ply it with grader and mower. Through processes of plant succession predictable by any botanist, the prairie garden becomes a refuge for quack grass. After the garden is gone, the highway department employs landscapers to dot the quack with elms, and with artistic clumps of Scotch pine, Japanese barberry, and Spiraea. Conservation Committees, en route to some important convention, whiz by and applaud this zeal for roadside beauty.

Some day we may need this prairie flora not only to look at but to rebuild the wasting soil of prairie farms. Many species may then be missing. We have our hearts in the right place, but we do not yet recognize the small cogs and wheels.

In our attempts to save the bigger cogs and wheels, we are still pretty naïve. A little repentance just before a species goes over the brink is enough to make us feel virtuous. When the species is gone we have a good cry and repeat the performance.

The recent extermination of the grizzly from most of the western stock-raising states is a case in point. Yes, we still have grizzlies in the Yellowstone. But the species is ridden by imported parasites; the rifles wait on every refuge boundary; new dude ranches and new roads constantly shrink the remaining range; every year sees fewer grizzlies on fewer ranges in fewer states. We console ourselves with the comfortable fallacy that a single museum-piece will do, ignoring the clear dictum of history that a species must be saved *in many places* if it is to be saved at all.

*   *   *

We need knowledge—public awareness—of the small cogs and wheels, but sometimes I think there is something we need even more. It is the thing that *Forest and Stream*, on its editorial masthead, once called 'a refined taste in natural objects.' Have we made any headway in developing 'a refined taste in natural objects'?

In the northern parts of the lake states we have

a few wolves left. Each state offers a bounty on wolves. In addition, it may invoke the expert services of the U.S. Fish and Wildlife Service in wolf-control. Yet both this agency and the several conservation commissions complain of an increasing number of localities where there are too many deer for the available feed. Foresters complain of periodic damage from too many rabbits. Why, then, continue the public policy of wolf-extermination? We debate such questions in terms of economics and biology. The mammalogists assert the wolf is the natural check on too many deer. The sportsmen reply they will take care of excess deer. Another decade of argument and there will be no wolves to argue about. One conservation inkpot cancels another.

In the lake states we are proud of our forest nurseries, and of the progress we are making in replanting what was once the north woods. But look in these nurseries and you will find no white cedar, no tamarack. Why no cedar? It grows too slowly, the deer eat it, the alders choke it. The prospect of a cedarless north woods does not depress our foresters; cedar has, in effect, been purged on grounds of economic inefficiency. For the same reason beech has been purged from the future forests of the Southeast. To these voluntary expungements of species from our future flora, we must add the involuntary ones arising from the importation of diseases: chestnut, persimmon, white pine. Is it sound economics to regard any plant as a separate entity, to proscribe or encourage it on the grounds of its individual performance? What will be the effect on animal life, on the soil, and on the health of the forest as an organism? 'A refined taste in natural objects' perceives that the economic issue is a separate consideration.

*   *   *

We who are the heirs and assigns of Paul Bunyan have not found out either what we are doing to the river or what the river is doing to us. We burl our logs of state with more energy than skill.

We have radically modified the biotic stream; we had to. Food chains now begin with corn and alfalfa instead of oaks and bluestem, flow through cows, hogs, and poultry instead of into elk, deer, and grouse, thence into farmers, flappers, and freshmen instead of Indians. That the flow is voluminous you can determine by consulting the telephone directory, or the roster of government agencies. The flow in this biotic stream is probably much greater than in the pre-Bunyan eras, but curiously enough science has never measured this.

Tame animals and plants have no tenacity as links in the new food chain; they are maintained, artificially, by the labor of farmers, aided by tractors, and abetted by a new kind of animal: the Professor of Agriculture. Paul Bunyan's burling was self-taught; now we have a 'prof' standing on the bank giving free instruction.

Each substitution of a tame plant or animal for a wild one, or an artificial waterway for a natural one, is accompanied by a readjustment in the circulating system of the land. We do not understand or foresee these readjustments; we are unconscious of them unless the end effect is bad. Whether it be the President rebuilding Florida for a ship canal, or Farmer Jones rebuilding a Wisconsin meadow for cow pasture, we are too busy with new tinkerings to think of end effects. That so many tinkerings are painless attests the youth and elasticity of the land organism.

One of the penalties of an ecological education is that one lives alone in a world of wounds. Much of the damage inflicted on land is quite invisible to laymen. An ecologist must either harden his shell and make believe that the consequences of science are none of his business, or he must be the doctor who sees the marks of death in a community that believes itself well and does not want to be told otherwise.

The government tells us we need flood control and comes to straighten the creek in our pasture. The engineer on the job tells us the creek is now able to carry off more flood water, but in the process we have lost our old willows where the owl hooted on a winter night and under which the cows switched flies in the noon shade. We lost the little marshy spot where our fringed gentians bloomed.

Hydrologists have demonstrated that the meanderings of a creek are a necessary part of the hydrologic functioning. The flood plain belongs to the river. The ecologist sees clearly that for similar reasons we can get along with less channel improvement on Round River.

Now to appraise the new order in terms of the two criteria: (1) Does it maintain fertility? (2) Does it maintain a diverse fauna and flora? Soils in the first stages of exploitation display a burst of plant and animal life. The abundant crops that evoked thanksgiving in the pioneers are well known, but there was also a burst of wild plants and animals. A score of imported food-bearing weeds had been added to the native flora, the soil was still rich, and landscape had been diversified by patches of plowland and pasture. The abundance of wildlife reported by the pioneers was in part the response to this diversity.

Such high metabolism is characteristic of newfound lands. It may represent normal circulation, or it may represent the combustion of stored fertility, i.e. biotic fever. One cannot distinguish the fever from normality by asking the biota to bite a thermometer. It can only be told *ex post facto* by the effect on the soil. What was the effect? The answer is written in gullies on a thousand fields. Crop yields per acre have remained about stationary. The vast technological improvements in farming have only offset the wastage in soil. In some regions, such as the dust bowl, the biotic stream has already shrunk below the point of navigability, and Paul's heirs have moved to California to ferment the grapes of wrath.

As for diversity, what remains of our native fauna and flora remains only because agriculture has not got around to destroying it. The present ideal of agriculture is clean farming; clean farming means a food chain aimed solely at economic profit and purged of all non-conforming links, a sort of *Pax Germanica* of the agricultural world. Diversity, on the other hand, means a food chain aimed to harmonize the wild and the tame in the joint interest of stability, productivity, and beauty.

Clean farming, to be sure, aspires to rebuild the soil, but it employs to this end only imported plants, animals, and fertilizers. It sees no need for the native flora and fauna that built the soil in the first place. Can stability be synthesized out of imported plants and animals? Is fertility that comes in sacks sufficient? These are the questions at issue.

No living man really knows. Testifying for the workability of clean farming is northeastern Europe, where a degree of biotic stability has been retained (except in humans) despite the wholesale artificialization of the landscape.

Testifying for its non-workability are all the other lands where it has ever been tried, including our own, and the tacit evidence of evolution, in which diversity and stability are so closely intertwined as to seem two names for one fact.

*   *   *

I had a bird dog named Gus. When Gus couldn't find pheasants he worked up an enthusiasm for Sora rails and meadowlarks. This whipped-up zeal for unsatisfactory substitutes masked his failure to find the real thing. It assuaged his inner frustration.

We conservationists are like that. We set out a generation ago to convince the American landowner to control fire, to grow forests, to manage wildlife. He did not respond very well. We have virtually no forestry, and mighty little range management, game management, wildflower management, pollution control, or erosion control being practiced voluntarily by private landowners. In many instances the abuse of private land is worse than it was before we started. If you don't believe that, watch the strawstacks burn on the Canadian prairies; watch the fertile mud flowing down the Rio Grande; watch the gullies climb the hillsides in the Palouse, in the Ozarks, in the riverbreaks of southern Iowa and western Wisconsin.

To assuage our inner frustration over this failure, we have found us a meadowlark. I don't know which dog first caught the scent; I do know that every dog on the field whipped into an enthusiastic backing-point. I did myself. The meadowlark was the idea that if the private landowner won't practice conservation, let's build a bureau to do it for him.

Like the meadowlark, this substitute has its good points. It smells like success. It is satisfactory on poor land which bureaus can buy. The trouble is that it contains no device for preventing good private land from becoming poor public land. There is danger in the assuagement of honest frustration; it helps us forget we have not yet found a pheasant.

I'm afraid the meadowlark is not going to remind us. He is flattered by his sudden importance.

*   *   *

Considering the prodigious achievements of the profit motive in wrecking land, one hesitates to reject it as a vehicle for restoring land. I incline to believe we have overestimated the scope of the profit motive. Is it profitable for the individual to build a beautiful home? To give his children a higher education? No, it is seldom profitable, yet we do both. These are, in fact, ethical and aesthetic premises which underlie the economic system. Once accepted, economic forces tend to align the smaller details of social organization into harmony with them.

No such ethical and aesthetic premise yet exists for the condition of the land these children must live in.

Our children are our signature to the roster of history; our land is merely the place our money was made. There is as yet no social stigma in the possession of a gullied farm, a wrecked forest, or a polluted stream, provided the dividends suffice to send the youngsters to college. Whatever ails the land, the government will fix it.

I think we have here the root of the problem. What conservation education must build is an ethical underpinning for land economics and a universal curiosity to understand the land mechanism. Conservation may then follow.

Natural History

One Saturday night not long ago, two middle-aged farmers set the alarm clock for a dark hour of what proved to be a snowy, blowy Sunday. Milking over, they jumped into a pickup and sped for the sand counties of central Wisconsin, a region productive of tax deeds, tamaracks, and wild hay. In the evening they returned with a truck full of young tamarack trees and a heart full of high adventure. The last tree was planted in the home marsh by lantern-light. There was still the milking.

In Wisconsin 'man bites dog' is stale news compared with 'farmer plants tamarack.' Our farmers have been grubbing, burning, draining, and chopping tamarack since 1840. In the region where these farmers live the tree is exterminated. Why then should they want to replace it? Because after twenty years they hope to reintroduce spagnum moss under the grove, and then lady's-slippers, pitcher plants, and the other nearly extinct wildflowers of the aboriginal Wisconsin bogs.

No extension bureau had offered these farmers any prize for this utterly quixotic undertaking. Certainly no hope of gain motivated it. How then can one interpret its meaning? I call it Revolt—revolt against the tedium of the merely economic attitude toward land. We assume that because we had to subjugate the land to live on it, the best farm is therefore the one most completely tamed. These two farmers have learned from experience that the wholly tamed farm offers not only a slender livelihood but a constricted life. They have caught the idea that there is pleasure to be had in raising wild crops as well as tame ones. They propose to devote a little spot of marsh to growing native wildflowers. Perhaps they wish for their land what we all wish for our children—not only a chance to make a living but also a chance to express and develop a rich and varied assortment of inherent capabilities, both wild and tame. What better expresses land than the plants that originally grew on it?

I talk here about the pleasure to be had in wild things, about natural-history studies as a combination sport and science.

History has not conspired to make my task an easy one. We naturalists have much to live down. There was a time when ladies and gentlemen wandered

afield not so much to learn how the world is put together as to gather subject matter for tea-time conversation. This was the era of dickey-bird ornithology,
of botany expressed in bad verse, of ejaculatory va-
pors such as 'ain't nature grand.' But if you will scan
the amateur ornithological or botanical journals of
today you will see that a new attitude is abroad.
But this is hardly the result of our present system of
formal education.

I know an industrial chemist who spends his spare
time reconstructing the history of the passenger pigeon
and its dramatic demise as a member of our fauna.
The pigeon became extinct before this chemist was
born, but he has dug up more knowledge of pigeons
than anyone had previously possessed. How? By reading every newspaper ever printed in our state, as
well as contemporary diaries, letters, and books. I
estimate that he has read 100,000 documents in his
search for pigeon data. This gigantic labor, which
would kill any man undertaking it as a task, fills him
with the keen delight of a hunter scouring the hills
for scarce deer, of an archeologist digging up Egypt
for a scarab. And of course such an undertaking requires more than digging. After the scarab is found
its interpretation requires the highest skill—a skill
not to be learned from others but rather to be developed by the digger as he digs. Here, then, is a
man who has found adventure, exploration, science,
and sport, all in the back yard of current history,
where millions of lesser men find only boredom.

Another exploration—this time literally of a back-
yard—is a study of the song sparrow conducted by
an Ohio housewife. This commonest of birds had been

scientifically labeled and classified a hundred years
ago, and forthwith forgotten. Our Ohio amateur had
the notion that in birds, as in people, there are
things to be known over and above name, sex, and
clothes. She began trapping the song sparrows in
her garden, marking each with a celluloid anklet,
and thus she was able to identify each individual
by its colored marker, to observe and record their
migrations, feedings, fightings, singings, matings,
nestings, and deaths; in short, to decipher the inner
workings of the sparrow community. In ten years
she knew more about sparrow society, sparrow politics, sparrow economics, and sparrow psychology
than anyone had ever learned about any bird. Science
beat a path to her door. Ornithologists of all nations
seek her counsel.

These two amateurs happen to have achieved
fame, but no thought of fame motivated their original work. Fame came *ex post facto*. It is not fame,
however, that I am talking about. They achieved
personal satisfactions which are more important than
fame, and hundreds of other amateurs are achieving
these satisfactions. I now ask: What is our educational system doing to encourage personal amateur
scholarship in the natural-history field? We can perhaps seek an answer to this question by dropping in
on a typical class in a typical zoology department. We
find there students memorizing the names of the
bumps on the bones of a cat. It is important, of
course, to study bones; otherwise we should never
comprehend the evolutionary process by which animals came into existence. But why memorize the
bumps? We are told that this is part of biological

discipline. I ask, though, whether a comprehension of the living animal and how it holds its place in the sun is not an equally important part. Unfortunately, the living animal is virtually omitted from the present

system of zoological education. In my own university, for example, we offer no course in ornithology or mammalogy.

Botanical education is in like case, except perhaps that the displacement of interest in the living flora has been not quite so extreme.

The reasons for this eviction of outdoor studies from the schools goes back into history. Laboratory biology came into existence at about the time when amateur natural history was of the dickey-bird variety, and when professional natural history consisted of labeling species and amassing facts about food habits without interpreting them. In short, a growing and vital laboratory technique was at that time placed in competition with a stagnated outdoor technique. It was quite natural that laboratory biology soon came to be regarded as the superior form of science. As it grew it crowded natural history out of the educational picture.

The present educational marathon in memorizing the geography of bones is the aftermath of this perfectly logical process of competition. It has, of course, other justifications. Medical students need it; zoology teachers need it. But I contend that the average citizen does not need it so badly as he needs some understanding of the living world.

In the interim, field studies have developed techniques and ideas quite as scientific as those of the laboratory. The amateur student is no longer confined to pleasant ambles in the country resulting merely in lists of species, lists of migration dates, and lists of raities. Bird banding, feather-marking, censusing, and experimental manipulations of behavior and environment are techniques available to all, and they are quantitative science. The amateur can, if he has imagination and persistence, select and solve actual scientific natural-history problems as virgin as the sun.

The modern view is to regard laboratory and field

not as competitive but rather as complementary studies. Curricula, however, do not yet reflect this new situation. It takes money to enlarge curricula, hence the average college student who inclines toward natural history avocations is rebuffed rather than encouraged by his university. Instead of being taught to see his native countryside with appreciation and intelligence, he is taught to carve cats. Let him be taught both if this is possible, but if one must be omitted let it be the latter.

To visualize more clearly the lopsidedness and sterility of biological education as a means of building citizens, let's go afield with some typical bright student and ask him some questions. We can safely assume he knows how plants grow and cats are put together, but let us test his comprehension of how the land is put together.

We are driving down a country road in northern Missouri. Here is a farmstead. Look at the trees in the yard and the soil in the field and tell us whether the original settler carved his farm out of prairie or woods. Did he eat prairie chicken or wild turkey for his Thanksgiving? What plants grew here originally which do not grow here now? Why did they disappear? What did the prairie plants have to do with creating the corn-yielding capacity of this soil? Why does this soil erode now but not then?

Again, suppose we are touring the Ozarks. Here is an abandoned field in which the ragweed is sparse and short. Does this tell us anything about why the mortgage was foreclosed? About how long ago? Would this field be a good place to look for quail? Does short ragweed have any connection with the human story behind yonder graveyard? If all the ragweed in this watershed were short, would that tell us anything about the future of floods in the stream? About the future prospects for bass or trout?

Many students would consider these questions insane, but they are not. Any amateur naturalist with

a seeing eye should be able to speculate intelligently on all of them, and have a lot of fun doing it. You will see, too, that modern natural history deals only incidentally with the identity of plants and animals, and only incidentally with their habits and behaviors. It deals principally with their relations to each other, their relation to the soil and water in which they grew, and their relations to the human beings who sing about 'my country' but see little or nothing of its inner workings. This science of relationships is called ecology, but what we call it matters nothing. The question is, does the educated citizen know he is only a cog in an ecological mechanism? That if he will work with that mechanism his mental wealth and his material wealth can expand indefinitely? But that if he refuses to work with it, it will ultimately grind him to dust? If education does not teach us these things, then what is education for?

We shall never achieve harmony with land, any more than we shall achieve absolute justice or liberty for people. In these higher aspirations the important thing is not to achieve, but to strive. It is only in mechanical enterprises that we can expect that early or complete fruition of effort which we call 'success.'

When we say 'striving,' we admit at the outset that the thing we need must grow from within. No striving for an idea was ever injected wholly from without.

The problem, then, is how to bring about a striving for harmony with land among a people many of whom have forgotten there is any such thing as land, among whom education and culture have become almost synonymous with landlessness. This is the problem of 'conservation education.'

Wildlife in American Culture

THE CULTURE of primitive peoples is often based on wildlife. Thus the plains Indian not only ate buffalo, but buffalo largely determined his architecture, dress, language, arts, and religion.

In civilized peoples the cultural base shifts elsewhere, but the culture nevertheless retains part of its wild roots. I here discuss the value of this wild rootage.

No one can weigh or measure culture, hence I shall waste no time trying to do so. Suffice it to say that by common consent of thinking people, there are cultural values in the sports, customs, and experiences that renew contacts with wild things. I venture the opinion that these values are of three kinds.

First there is value in any experience that reminds us of our distinctive national origins and evolution, i.e. that stimulates awareness of history. Such awareness is 'nationalism' in its best sense. For lack of any other short name, I shall call this, in our case, the 'split-rail value.' For example: a boy scout has tanned a coonskin cap, and goes Daniel-Booneing in the willow thicket below the tracks. He is reenacting American history. He is, to that extent, culturally prepared to face the dark and bloody realities of the present. Again: a farmer boy arrives in the schoolroom reeking of muskrat; he has tended his traps

before breakfast. He is reenacting the romance of the
fur trade. Ontogeny repeats phylogeny in society as
well as in the individual.

Second, there is value in any experience that reminds us of our dependency on the soil-plant-animal-
man food chain, and of the fundamental organization of the biota. Civilization has so cluttered this
elemental man-earth relation with gadgets and middlemen that awareness of it is growing dim. We
fancy that industry supports us, forgetting what supports industry. Time was when education moved
toward soil, not away from it. The nursery jingle
about bringing home a rabbit skin to wrap the baby
bunting in is one of many reminders in folk-lore that
man once hunted to feed and clothe his family.

Third, there is value in any experience that exercises those ethical restraints collectively called 'sportsmanship.' Our tools for the pursuit of wildlife improve faster than we do, and sportsmanship is a
voluntary limitation in the use of these armaments.
It is aimed to augment the role of skill and shrink
the role of gadgets in the pursuit of wild things.

A peculiar virtue in wildlife ethics is that the
hunter ordinarily has no gallery to applaud or dis-
approve of his conduct. Whatever his acts, they are
dictated by his own conscience, rather than by a mob
of onlookers. It is difficult to exaggerate the importance of this fact.

Voluntary adherence to an ethical code elevates the
self-respect of the sportsman, but it should not be
forgotten that voluntary disregard of the code de-
generates and depraves him. For example, a common
denominator of all sporting codes is not to waste

good meat. Yet it is now a demonstrable fact that Wisconsin deer-hunters, in their pursuit of a legal buck, kill and abandon in the woods at least one doe, fawn, or spike buck for every two legal bucks taken out. In other words, approximately half the hunters shoot any deer until a legal deer is killed. The illegal carcasses are left where they fall. Such deer-hunting is not only without social value, but constitutes actual training for ethical depravity elsewhere.

It seems, then, that split-rail and man-earth experiences have zero or plus values, but that ethical experiences may have minus values as well.

This, then, defines roughly three kinds of cultural nutriment available to our outdoor roots. It does not follow that culture is fed. The extraction of value is never automatic; only a healthy culture can feed and grow. Is culture fed by our present forms of outdoor recreation?

The pioneer period gave birth to two ideas that are the essence of split-rail value in outdoor sports. One is the 'go-light' idea, the other the 'one-bullet-one-buck' idea. The pioneer went light of necessity. He shot with economy and precision because he lacked the transport, the cash, and the weapons requisite for machine-gun tactics. Let it be clear, then, that in their inception, both of these ideas were forced on us; we made a virtue of necessity.

In their later evolution, however, they became a code of sportsmanship, a self-imposed limitation on sport. On them is based a distinctively American tradition of self-reliance, hardihood, woodcraft, and marksmanship. These are intangibles, but they are not abstractions. Theodore Roosevelt was a great sportsman, not because he hung up many trophies, but because he expressed this intangible American tradition in words any schoolboy could understand. A more subtle and accurate expression is found in the early writings of Stewart Edward White. It is not far amiss to say that such men created cultural value by being aware of it, and by creating a pattern for its growth.

Then came the gadgeteer, otherwise known as the sporting-goods dealer. He has draped the American outdoorsman with an infinity of contraptions, all offered as aids to self-reliance, hardihood, woodcraft, or marksmanship, but too often functioning as sub stitutes for them. Gadgets fill the pockets, they dangle from neck and belt. The overflow fills the auto-trunk, and also the trailer. Each item of outdoor equipment grows lighter and often better, but the aggregate poundage becomes tonnage. The traffic in gadgets adds up to astronomical sums, which are soberly published as representing 'the economic value of wildlife.' But what of cultural values?

As an end-case consider the duck-hunter, sitting in a steel boat behind composition decoys. A put-put motor has brought him to the blind without exercise. Canned heat stands by to warm him in case of a chilling wind. He talks to the passing flocks on a factory caller, in what he hopes are seductive tones; home lessons from a phonograph record have taught him how. The decoys work, despite the caller; a flock circles in. It must be shot at before it circles twice, for the marsh bristles with other sportsmen, similarly accoutred, who might shoot first. He opens up at 70

yards, for his polychoke is set for infinity, and the advertisements have told him that Super-Z shells, and plenty of them, have a long reach. The flock flares. A couple of cripples scale off to die elsewhere. Is this sportsman absorbing cultural value? Or is he just feeding minks? The next blind opens up at 75 yards; how else is a fellow to get some shooting? This is duck shooting, current model. It is typical of all public grounds, and of many clubs. Where is the go-light idea, the one-bullet tradition?

The answer is not a simple one. Roosevelt did not disdain the modern rifle; White used freely the aluminum pot, the silk tent, dehydrated foods. Somehow they used mechanical aids, in moderation, without being used by them.

I do not pretend to know what is moderation, or where the line is between legitimate and illegitimate gadgets. It seems clear, though, that the origin of gadgets has much to do with their cultural effects. Homemade aids to sport or outdoor life often enhance, rather than destroy, the man-earth drama; he who kills a trout with his own fly has scored two coups, not one. I use many factory-made gadgets myself. Yet there must be some limit beyond which money-bought aids to sport destroy the cultural value of sport.

Not all sports have degenerated to the same extent as duck-hunting. Defenders of the American tradition still exists. Perhaps the bow-and-arrow movement and the revival of falconry mark the beginnings of a reaction. The net trend, however, is clearly toward more and more mechanization, with a corresponding shrinkage in cultural values, especially split-rail values and ethical restraints.

I have the impression that the American sportsman is puzzled; he doesn't understand what is happening to him. Bigger and better gadgets are good for industry, so why not for outdoor recreation? It has not dawned on him that outdoor recreations are essentially primitive, atavistic; that their value is a contrast-value; that excessive mechanization destroys contrasts by moving the factory to the woods or to the marsh.

The sportsman has no leaders to tell him what is wrong. The sporting press no longer represents sport; it has turned billboard for the gadgeteer. Wildlife administrators are too busy producing something to shoot at to worry much about the cultural value of the shooting. Because everybody from Xenophon to Teddy Roosevelt said sport has value, it is assumed that this value must be indestructible.

Among non-gunpowder sports, the impact of mechanization has had diverse effects. The modern field glass, camera, and the aluminum bird-band have certainly *not* deteriorated the cultural value of ornithology. Fishing, but for outboard motors and aluminum canoes, seems less severely mechanized than hunting. On the other hand, motorized transport has nearly destroyed the sport of wilderness travel by leaving only fly-specks of wilderness to travel in.

Fox-hunting with hounds, backwoods style, presents a dramatic instance of partial and perhaps harmless mechanized invasion. This is one of the purest of sports; it has real split-rail flavor; it has man-earth drama of the first water. The fox is deliberately left unshot, hence ethical restraint is also present. But we now follow the chase in Fords! The voice of Bugle Ann mingles with the honk of the flivver! However, no one is likely to invent a mechanical foxhound, or to screw a polychoke on the hound's nose. No one is likely to teach dog-training by phonograph, or by other painless shortcuts. I think the gadgeteer has reached the end of his tether in dogdom.

It is not quite accurate to ascribe all the ills of sport to the inventor of physical aids-to-sport. The advertiser invents ideas, and ideas are seldom as honest as physical objects, even though they may be equally useless. One such deserves special mention: the 'where-to-go' department. Knowledge of the whereabouts of good hunting or fishing is a very personal form of property. It is like rod, dog, or gun: a thing to be loaned or given as a personal courtesy. But to hawk it in the marketplace of the sports column as an aid to circulation seems to me another matter. To hand it to all and sundry as free public 'service' seems to me distinctly another matter. Even 'conservation' departments now tell Tom, Dick, and Harry where the fish are biting, and where a flock of ducks has ventured to alight for a meal.

All of these organized promiscuities tend to depersonalize one of the essentially personal elements in outdoor sports. I do not know where the line lies between legitimate and illegitimate practice; I am convinced, though, that 'where-to-go' service has broken all bounds of reason.

If the hunting or fishing is good, the 'where-to-go' service suffices to attract the desired excess of sportsmen. But if it is no good, the advertiser must resort to more forcible means. One such is the fishing lottery, in which a few hatchery fish are tagged, and a prize is offered for the fisherman catching the winning number. This curious hybrid between the techniques of science and of the pool hall insures the overfishing of many an already exhausted lake, and brings a glow of civic pride to many a village Chamber of Commerce.

It is idle for the professional wildlife managers to consider themselves aloof from these affairs. The production engineer and the salesman belong to the same company; both are tarred with the same stick.

Wildlife managers are trying to raise game in the wild by manipulating its environment, and thus to convert hunting from exploitation to cropping. If the conversion takes place, how will it affect cultural values? It must be admitted that split-rail flavor and free-for-all exploitation are historically associated. Daniel Boone had scant patience with agricultural cropping, let alone wildlife cropping. Perhaps the stubborn reluctance of the 'one-gallus' sportsman to be converted to the cropping idea is an expression of his split-rail inheritance. Probably cropping is resisted because it is incompatible with one component of the split-rail tradition: free hunting.

Mechanization offers no cultural substitute for the split-rail values it destroys; at least none visible to me. Cropping or management does offer a substitute, which to me has at least equal value: wild husbandry. The experience of managing land for wildlife crops has the same value as any other form of farming; it is a reminder of the man-earth relation. Moreover ethical restraints are involved; thus managing game without resorting to predator-control calls for ethical restraint of a high order. It may be concluded, then, that game cropping shrinks one value (split-rail) but enhances both of the others.

If we regard outdoor sports as a field of conflict between an immensely vigorous process of mechanization and a wholly static tradition, then the outlook for cultural values is indeed dark. But why cannot our concept of sport grow with the same vigor as our list of gadgets? Perhaps the salvation of cultural value lies in seizing the offensive. I, for one, believe that the time is ripe. Sportsmen can determine for themselves the shape of things to come.

The last decade, for example, has disclosed a totally new form of sport, which does not destroy wildlife, which uses gadgets without being used by them, which outflanks the problem of posted land, and which greatly increases the human carrying capacity of a unit area. This sport knows no bag limit, no closed season. It needs teachers, but not wardens. It calls for a new woodcraft of the highest cultural value. The sport I refer to is wildlife research.

Wildlife research started as a professional priest-craft. The more difficult and laborious research problems must doubtless remain in professional hands, but there are plenty of problems suitable for all grades of amateurs. In the field of mechanical invention research has long since spread to amateurs. In the biological field the sport-value of amateur research is just beginning to be realized.

Thus Margaret Morse Nice, an amateur ornithologist, studied song sparrows in her back yard. She has become a world-authority on bird behavior, and has out-thought and outworked many a professional student of social organization in birds. Charles L. Broley, a banker, banded eagles for fun. He discovered a hitherto unknown fact: that some eagles nest in the South in winter, and then go vacationing to the north woods. Norman and Stuart Criddle, wheat ranchers on the Manitoba prairies, studied the fauna and flora of their farm, and became recognized authorities on everything from local botany to wild-life cycles. Elliott S. Barker, a cowman in the New Mexico mountains, has written one of the two best books on that elusive cat: the mountain lion. Do not let anyone tell you that these people made work out of play. They simply realized that the most fun lies in seeing and studying the unknown.

Ornithology, mammalogy, and botany, as now known to most amateurs, are but kindergarten games compared with what is possible for (and open to) amateurs in these fields. One reason for this is that the whole structure of biological education (including education in wildlife) is aimed to perpetuate the professional monopoly on research. To the amateur are allotted only make-believe voyages of discovery, to verify what professional authority already knows. What the youth needs to be told is that a ship is a-building in his own mental dry dock, a ship with freedom of the seas.

In my opinion, the promotion of wildlife research sports is the most important job confronting the profession of wildlife management. Wildlife has still another value, now visible only to a few ecologists, but of potential importance to the whole human enterprise.

We now know that animal populations have behavior patterns of which the individual animal is unaware, but which he nevertheless helps to excute. Thus the rabbit is unaware of cycles, but he is the vehicle for cycles.

We cannot discern these behavior patterns in the individual, or in short periods of time. The most intense scrutiny of an individual rabbit tells us nothing of cycles. The cycle concept springs from a scrutiny the mass through decades.

This raises the disquieting question: do human populations have behavior patterns of which we are unaware, but which we help to excute? Are mobs and wars, unrests and revolutions, cut of such cloth?

Many historians and philosophers persist in interpreting our mass behaviors as the collective result of individual acts of volition. The whole subject matter of diplomacy assumes that the political group has the properties of an honorable person. On the other hand, some economists see the whole of society as a plaything for processes, our knowledge of which is largely *ex post facto*.

It is reasonable to suppose that our social processes have a higher volitional content that those of the rabbit, but it is also reasonable to suppose that we, as a species, contain population behavior patterns of which nothing is known because circumstance has never evoked them. We may have others the meaning of which we have misread.

This state of doubt about the fundamentals of human population behavior lends exceptional interest, and exceptional value, to the only available analogue: the higher animals. Errington, among others, has pointed out the cultural value of these animal annalogues. For centuries this rich library of knowledge has been inaccessible to us because we did not know where or how to look for it. Ecology is now teaching us to search in animal populations for analogies to our own problems. By learning how some small part of the biota ticks, we can guess how the whole mechanism ticks. The ability to perceive these deeper meanings, and to appraise them critically, is the woodcraft of the future.

To sum up, wildlife once fed us and shaped our culture. It still yields us pleasure for leisure hours, but we try to reap that pleasure by modern machinery and thus destroy part of its value. Reaping it by modern mentality would yield not only pleasure, but wisdom as well.

The Deer Swath

ONE HOT afternoon in August I sat under the elm, idling, when I saw a deer pass across a small opening a quarter mile east. A deer trail crosses our farm, and at this point any deer traveling is briefly visible from the shack.

I then realized that half an hour before I had moved my chair to the best spot for watching the deer trail; that I had done this habitually for years, without being clearly conscious of it. This led to the thought that by cutting some brush I could widen the zone of visibility. Before night the swath was cleared, and within the month I detected several deer which otherwise could likely have passed unseen.

The new deer swath was pointed out to a series of weekend guests for the purpose of watching their later reactions to it. It was soon clear that most of them forgot it quickly, while others watched it, as I did, whenever chance allowed. The upshot was the realization that there are four categories of outdoors men: deer hunters, duck hunters, bird hunters, and non-hunters. These categories have nothing to do with sex or age, or accountrements; they represent four diverse habits of the human eye. The deer hunter habitually watches the next bend; the duck hunter

watches the skyline; the bird hunter watches the dog; the non-hunter does not watch.

When the deer hunter sits down he sits where he can see ahead, and with his back to something. The duck hunter sits where he can see overhead, and behind something. The non-hunter sits where he is comfortable. None of these watches the dog. The bird hunter watches only the dog, and always knows where the dog is, whether or not visible at the moment. The dog's nose is the bird hunter's eye. Many hunters who carry a shotgun in season have never learned to watch the dog, or to interpret his reactions to scent.

There are good outdoors men who do not conform to these categories. There is the ornithologist who hunts by ear, and uses the eye only to follow up on what his ear has detected. There is the botanist who hunts by eye, but at much closer range; he is a marvel at finding plants, but seldom sees birds or mammals. There is the forester who sees only trees, and the insects and fungi that prey upon trees; he is oblivious to all else. And finally there is the sportsman who sees only game, and regards all else as of little interest or value.

There is one illusive mode of hunting which I cannot associate exclusively with any of these groups: the search for scats, tracks, feathers, dens, roostings, rubbings, dustings, diggings, feedings, fightings, or preyings collectively known to woodsmen as 'reading sign.' This skill is rare, and too often seems to be inverse to book learning.

The counterpart of reading animal sign exists in the plant field, but skill is equally rare in occurrence and illusive in distribution. To prove this I cite the African explorer who detected the scratchings of a lion on the bark of a tree, 20 feet up. The scratchings, he said, had been made when the tree was young.

The biological jack-of-all-trades called ecologist tries to be and do all these things. Needless to say, he does not succeed.

Goose Music

SOME YEARS ago the game of golf was commonly regarded in this country as a kind of social ornament, a pretty diversion for the idle rich, but hardly worthy of the curiosity, much less of the serious interest, of men of affairs. Today scores of cities are building municipal golf courses to make golf available to the rank and file of their citizens.

The same change in point of view has occurred toward most other outdoor sports—the frivolities of fifty years ago have become the social necessities of today. But strangely enough, this change is only just beginning to permeate our attitude toward the oldest and most universal of all sports, hunting and fishing.

We have realized dimly, of course, that a day afield was good for the tired businessman. We have also realized that the destruction of wildlife removed the incentive for days afield. But we have not yet learned to express the value of wildlife in terms of social welfare. Some have attempted to justify wildlife conservation in terms of meat, others in terms of personal pleasure, others in terms of cash, still others in the interest of science, education, agriculture, art, public health, and even military preparedness. But few have so far clearly realized and expressed the whole truth, namely, that all these things are but factors in a broad social value, and that wildlife, like golf, is a social asset.

But to those whose hearts are stirred by the sound of whistling wings and quacking mallards, wildlife is something even more than this. It is not merely an acquired taste; the instinct that finds delight in the sight and pursuit of game is bred into the very fiber of the race. Golf is sophisticated exercise, but the love of hunting is almost a physiological characteristic. A man may not care for golf and still be human, but the man who does not like to see, hunt, photograph, or otherwise outwit birds or animals is hardly normal. He is supercivilized, and I for one do not know how to deal with him. Babes do not tremble when they are shown a golf ball, but I should not like to own the boy whose hair does not lift his hat when he sees his first deer. We are dealing, therefore, with something that lies very deep. Some can live without opportunity for the exercise and control of the hunting instinct, just as I suppose some can live without work, play, love, business, or other vital adventure. But in these days we regard such deprivations as unsocial. Opportunity for exercise of all the normal instincts has come to be regarded more and more as an inalienable right. The men who are destroying our wildlife are alienating one of these rights, and doing a thorough job of it. More than that, they are doing a permanent job of it. When the last corner lot is covered with tenements we can still make a playground by tearing them down, but when the last antelope goes by the board, not all the playground associations in Christendom can do aught to replace the loss.

If wild birds and animals are a social asset, how much of an asset are they? It is easy to say that some of us, afflicted with hereditary hunting fever, cannot live satisfactory lives without them. But this does

not establish any comparative value, and in these days it is sometimes necessary to choose between necessities. In short, what is a wild goose worth? I have a ticket to the symphony. It was not cheap. The dollars were well spent, but I would forgo the experience for the sight of the big gander that sailed honking into my decoys at daybreak this morning. It was bitter cold and I was all thumbs, so I blithely missed him. But miss or no miss, I saw him, I heard the wind whistle through his set wings as he came honking out of the gray west, and I felt him so that even now I tingle at the recollection. I doubt not that this very gander has given ten other men a symphony ticket's worth of thrills.

My notes tell me I have seen a thousand geese this fall. Every one of these in the course of their epic journey from the arctic to the gulf has on one occasion or another probably served man in some equivalent of paid entertainment. One flock perhaps has thrilled a score of schoolboys, and sent them scurrying home with tales of high adventure. Another, passing overhead of a dark night, has serenaded a whole city with goose music, and awakened who knows what questionings and memories and hopes. A third perhaps has given pause to some farmer at his plow, and brought new thoughts of far lands and journeyings and peoples, where before was only drudgery, barren of any thought at all. I am sure those thousand geese are paying human dividends on a dollar value. Worth in dollars is only an exchange value, like the sale value of a painting or the copyright of a poem. What about the replacement value? Supposing there were no longer any painting, or poetry, or goose music? It is a black thought to dwell upon, but it must be answered. In dire necessity somebody might write another *Iliad*, or paint an 'Angelus,' but fashion a goose? 'I, the Lord, will answer them. The hand of the Lord hath done this, and the Holy One of Israel created it.'

Is it impious to weigh goose music and art in the same scales? I think not, because the true hunter is merely a noncreative artist. Who painted the first picture on a bone in the caves of France? A hunter. Who alone in our modern life so thrills to the sight of living beauty that he will endure hunger and thirst and cold to feed his eye upon it? The hunter. Who wrote the great hunter's poem about the sheer wonder of the wind, the hail, and the snow, the stars, the lightnings, and the clouds, the lion, the deer, and the wild goat, the raven, the hawk, and the eagle, and above all the eulogy of the horse? Job, one of the great dramatic artists of all time. Poets sing and hunters scale the mountains primarily for one and the same reason—the thrill to beauty. Critics write and hunters outwit their game primarily for one and the same reason—to reduce that beauty to possession. The differences are largely matters of degree, consciousness, and that sly arbiter of the classification of human activities, language. If, then, we can live without goose music, we may as well do away with stars, or sunsets, or Iliads. But the point is that we would be fools to do away with any of them.

What value has wildlife from the standpoint of morals and religion? I heard of a boy once who was brought up an atheist. He changed his mind when he saw that there were a hundred-odd species of warblers, each bedecked like to the rainbow, and each performing yearly sundry thousands of miles of migration about which scientists wrote wisely but did not understand. No 'fortuitous concourse of elements' working blindly through any number of millions of years could quite account for why warblers are so beautiful. No mechanistic theory, even bolstered by muta-

tions, has ever quite answered for the colors of the cerulean warbler, or the vespers of the woodthrush, or the swansong, or—goose music. I dare say this boy's convictions would be harder to shake than those of many inductive theologians. There are yet many boys to be born who, like Isaiah, 'may see, and know, and consider, and understand together, that the hand of the Lord hath done this. But where shall they see, and know, and consider? In museums?

What is the effect of hunting and fishing on character as compared with other outdoor sports? I have already pointed out that the desire lies deeper, that its source is a matter of instinct as well as of competition. A son of a Robinson Crusoe, having never seen a tennis racket, might get along nicely without one, but he would be pretty sure to hunt or fish whether or not he were taught to do so. But this does not establish any superiority as to subjective benefits. Which helps the more to build a man? This question (like the one we used to debate in school about whether boys or girls are the best scholars) might be argued till doomsday. I shall not attempt it. But there are two points about hunting that deserve special emphasis. One is that the ethics of sportsmanship is not a fixed code, but must be formulated and practiced by the individual, with no referee but the Almighty. The other is that hunting generally involves the handling of dogs and horses, and the lack of this experience is one of the most serious defects of our gasoline-driven civilization. There was much truth in the old idea that any man ignorant of dogs and horses was not a gentleman. In the West the abuse of horses is still a universal blackball. This rule of thumb was adopted in the cow country long before 'character analysis' was invented and, for all we know, may yet outlive it.

But after all, it is poor business to prove that one good thing is better than another. The point is that some six or eight millions of Americans like to hunt and fish, that the hunting fever is endemic in the race, that the race is benefited by any incentive to get out into the open, and is being injured by the destruction of the incentive in this case. To combat this destruction is therefore a social issue.

To conclude: I have congenital hunting fever and three sons. As little tots, they spent their time playing with my decoys and scouring vacant lots with wooden guns. I hope to leave them good health, an education, and possibly even a competence. But what are they going to do with these things if there be no more deer in the hills, and no more quail in the coverts? No more snipe whistling in the meadow, no more piping of widgeons and chattering of teal as darkness covers the marshes; no more whistling of swift wings when the morning star pales in the east? And when the dawn-wind stirs through the ancient cottonwoods, and the gray light steals down from the hills over the old river sliding softly past its wide brown sand-bars—what if there be no more goose music?

Part IV
The Upshot

The Land Ethic

WHEN GOD-LIKE Odysseus returned from the wars in Troy, he hanged all on one rope a dozen slave-girls of his household whom he suspected of misbehavior during his absence.

This hanging involved no question of propriety. The girls were property. The disposal of property was then, as now, a matter of expediency, not of right and wrong.

Concepts of right and wrong were not lacking from Odysseus' Greece: witness the fidelity of his wife through the long years before at last his black-prowed galleys clove the wine-dark seas for home. The ethical structure of that day covered wives, but had not yet been extended to human chattels. During the three thousand years which have since elapsed, ethical criteria have been extended to many fields of conduct, with corresponding shrinkages in those judged by expediency only.

The Ethical Sequence

This extension of ethics, so far studied only by
philosophers, is actually a process in ecological evolution. Its sequences may be described in ecological as
well as in philosophical terms. An ethic, ecologically,
is a limitation on freedom of action in the struggle for
existence. An ethic, philosophically, is a differentia-
tion of social from anti-social conduct. These are two
definitions of one thing. The thing has its origin in
the tendency of interdependent individuals or groups
to evolve modes of co-operation. The ecologist calls
these symbioses. Politics and economics are advanced
symbioses in which the original free-for-all competition has been replaced, in part, by co-operative
mechanisms with an ethical content.

The complexity of co-operative mechanisms has
increased with population density, and with the efficiency of tools. It was simpler, for example, to define
the anti-social uses of sticks and stones in the days
of the mastodons than of bullets and billboards in the
age of motors.

The first ethics dealt with the relation between
individuals; the Mosaic Decalogue is an example.
Later accretions dealt with the relation between the
individual and society. The Golden Rule tries to integrate the individual to society; democracy to integrate
social organization to the individual.

There is as yet no ethic dealing with man's relation to land and to the animals and plants which
grow upon it. Land, like Odysseus' slave-girls, is still
property. The land-relation is still strictly economic,
entailing privileges but not obligations.

The extension of ethics to this third element in human environment is, if I read the evidence correctly, an evolutionary possibility and an ecological necessity. It is the third step in a sequence. The first two have already been taken. Individual thinkers since the days of Ezekiel and Isaiah have asserted that the despoliation of land is not only inexpedient but wrong. Society, however, has not yet affirmed their belief. I regard the present conservation movement as the embryo of such an affirmation.

An ethic may be regarded as a mode of guidance for meeting ecological situations so new or intricate, or involving such deferred reactions, that the path of social expediency is not discernible to the average individual. Animal instincts are modes of guidance for the individual in meeting such situations. Ethics are possibly a kind of community instinct in-the-making.

The Community Concept

All ethics so far evolved rest upon a single premise: that the individual is a member of a community of interdependent parts. His instincts prompt him to compete for his place in the community, but his ethics prompt him also to co-operate (perhaps in order that there may be a place to compete for).

The land ethic simply enlarges the boundaries of the community to include soils, waters, plants, and animals, or collectively: the land.

This sounds simple: do we not already sing our love for and obligation to the land of the free and the home of the brave? Yes, but just what and whom do we love? Certainly not the soil, which we are sending helter-skelter downriver. Certainly not the waters, which we assume have no function except to turn turbines, float barges, and carry off sewage. Certainly not the plants, of which we exterminate whole communities without batting an eye. Certainly not the animals, of which we have already extirpated many of the largest and most beautiful species. A land ethic of course cannot prevent the alteration, management, and use of these 'resources,' but it does affirm their right to continued existence, and, at least in spots, their continued existence in a natural state.

In short, a land ethic changes the role of *Homo sapiens* from conqueror of the land-community to plain member and citizen of it. It implies respect for his fellow-members, and also respect for the community as such.

In human history, we have learned (I hope) that the conqueror role is eventually self-defeating. Why? Because it is implicit in such a role that the conqueror knows, *ex cathedra*, just what makes the community clock tick, and just what and who is valuable, and what and who is worthless, in community life. It always turns out that he knows neither, and this is why his conquests eventually defeat themselves.

In the biotic community, a parallel situation exists. Abraham knew exactly what the land was for: it was to drip milk and honey into Abraham's mouth. At the present moment, the assurance with which we regard this assumption is inverse to the degree of our education.

The ordinary citizen today assumes that science

knows what makes the community clock tick; the scientist is equally sure that he does not. He knows that the biotic mechanism is so complex that its workings may never be fully understood.

That man is, in fact, only a member of a biotic team is shown by an ecological interpretation of history. Many historical events, hitherto explained solely in terms of human enterprise, were actually biotic interactions between people and land. The characteristics of the land determined the facts quite as potently as the characteristics of the men who lived on it.

Consider, for example, the settlement of the Mississippi valley. In the years following the Revolution, three groups were contending for its control: the native Indian, the French and English traders, and the American settlers. Historians wonder what would have happened if the English at Detroit had thrown a little more weight into the Indian side of those tipsy scales which decided the outcome of the colonial migration into the cane-lands of Kentucky. It is time now to ponder the fact that the cane-lands, when subjected to the particular mixture of forces represented by the cow, plow, fire, and axe of the pioneer, became bluegrass. What if the plant succession inherent in this dark and bloody ground had, under the impact of these forces, given us some worthless sedge, shrub, or weed? Would Boone and Kenton have held out? Would there have been any overflow into Ohio, Indiana, Illinois, and Missouri? Any Louisiana Purchase? Any transcontinental union of new states? Any Civil War?

Kentucky was one sentence in the drama of history.

We are commonly told what the human actors in this drama tried to do, but we are seldom told that their success, or the lack of it, hung in large degree on the reaction of particular soils to the impact of the particular forces exerted by their occupancy. In the case of Kentucky, we do not even know where the bluegrass came from—whether it is a native species, or a stowaway from Europe.

Contrast the cane-lands with what hindsight tells us about the Southwest, where the pioneers were equally brave, resourceful, and persevering. The impact of occupancy here brought no bluegrass, or other plant fitted to withstand the bumps and buffetings of hard use. This region, when grazed by livestock, reverted through a series of more and more worthless grasses, shrubs, and weeds to a condition of unstable equilibrium. Each recession of plant types bred erosion; each increment to erosion bred a further recession of plants. The result today is a progressive and mutual deterioration, not only of plants and soils, but of the animal community subsisting thereon. The early settlers did not expect this: on the ciénegas of New Mexico some even cut ditches to hasten it. So subtle has been its progress that few residents of the region are aware of it. It is quite invisible to the tourist who finds this wrecked landscape colorful and charming (as indeed it is, but it bears scant resemblance to what it was in 1848).

This same landscape was 'developed' once before, but with quite different results. The Pueblo Indians settled the Southwest in pre-Columbian times, but they happened *not* to be equipped with range livestock. Their civilization expired, but not because their land expired.

In India, regions devoid of any sod-forming grass have been settled, apparently without wrecking the land, by the simple expedient of carrying the grass to the cow, rather than vice versa. (Was this the result of some deep wisdom, or was it just good luck? I do not know.)

In short, the plant succession steered the course of history; the pioneer simply demonstrated, for good or ill, what successions inhered in the land. Is history taught in this spirit? It will be, once the concept of land as a community really penetrates our intellectual life.

The Ecological Conscience

Conservation is a state of harmony between men and land. Despite nearly a century of propaganda, conservation still proceeds at a snail's pace; progress still consists largely of letterhead pieties and convention oratory. On the back forty we still slip two steps backward for each forward stride.

The usual answer to this dilemma is 'more conservation education.' No one will debate this, but is it certain that only the *volume* of education needs stepping up? Is something lacking in the *content* as well?

It is difficult to give a fair summary of its content in brief form, but, as I understand it, the content is substantially this: obey the law, vote right, join some organizations, and practice what conservation is profitable on your own land; the government will do the rest.

Is not this formula too easy to accomplish anything worth-while? It defines no right or wrong, assigns no obligation, calls for no sacrifice, implies no change in the current philosophy of values. In respect of land-use, it urges only enlightened self-interest. Just how far will such education take us? An example will perhaps yield a partial answer.

By 1930 it had become clear to all except the ecologically blind that southwestern Wisconsin's topsoil was slipping seaward. In 1933 the farmers were told that if they would adopt certain remedial practices for five years, the public would donate CCC labor to install them, plus the necessary machinery and materials. The offer was widely accepted, but the practices were widely forgotten when the five-year contract period was up. The farmers continued only those practices that yielded an immediate and visible economic gain for themselves.

This led to the idea that maybe farmers would learn more quickly if they themselves wrote the rules. Accordingly the Wisconsin Legislature in 1937 passed the Soil Conservation District Law. This said to farmers, in effect: *We, the public, will furnish you free technical service and loan you specialized machinery, if you will write your own rules for land-use. Each county may write its own rules, and these will have the force of* law. Nearly all the counties promptly organized to accept the proffered help, but after a decade of operation, *no county has yet written a single rule*. There has been visible progress in such practices as strip-cropping, pasture renovation, and soil liming, but none in fencing woodlots against grazing, and none in excluding plow and cow from steep slopes. The farmers, in short, have selected those remedial practices which were profitable anyhow, and ignored those which were profitable to the community, but not clearly profitable to themselves.

When one asks why no rules have been written, one is told that the community is not yet ready to support them; education must precede rules. But the education actually in progress makes no mention of obligations to land over and above those dictated by self-interest. The net result is that we have more education but less soil, fewer healthy woods, and as many floods as in 1937.

The puzzling aspect of such situations is that the existence of obligations over and above self-interest is taken for granted in such rural community enterprises as the betterment of roads, schools, churches, and baseball teams. Their existence is not taken for granted, nor as yet seriously discussed, in bettering the behavior of the water that falls on the land, or in the preserving of the beauty or diversity of the farm landscape. Land-use ethics are still governed wholly by economic self-interest, just as social ethics were a century ago.

To sum up: we asked the farmer to do what he conveniently could to save his soil, and he has done just that, and only that. The farmer who clears the woods off a 75 per cent slope, turns his cows into the clearing, and dumps its rainfall, rocks, and soil into the community creek, is still (if otherwise decent) a respected member of society. If he puts lime on his fields and plants his crops on contour, he is still entitled to all the privileges and emoluments of his Soil Conservation District. The District is a beautiful piece of social machinery, but it is coughing along on two cylinders because we have been too timid, and too anxious for quick success, to tell the farmer the true magnitude of his obligations. Obligations have no meaning without conscience, and the problem we face is the extension of the social conscience from people to land.

No important change in ethics was ever accomplished without an internal change in our intellectual emphasis, loyalties, affections, and convictions. The proof that conservation has not yet touched these foundations of conduct lies in the fact that philosophy and religion have not yet heard of it. In our attempt to make conservation easy, we have made it trivial.

Substitutes for a Land Ethic

When the logic of history hungers for bread and we hand out a stone, we are at pains to explain how much the stone resembles bread. I now describe some of the stones which serve in lieu of a land ethic.

One basic weakness in a conservation system based wholly on economic motives is that most members of the land community have no economic value. Wildflowers and songbirds are examples. Of the 22,000 higher plants and animals native to Wisconsin, it is doubtful whether more than 5 per cent can be sold, fed, eaten, or otherwise put to economic use. Yet these creatures are members of the biotic community, and if (as I believe) its stability depends on its integrity, they are entitled to continuance.

When one of these non-economic categories is threatened, and if we happen to love it, we invent subterfuges to give it economic importance. At the beginning of the century songbirds were supposed to be disappearing. Ornithologists jumped to the rescue with some distinctly shaky evidence to the effect that insects would eat us up if birds failed to control them. The evidence had to be economic in order to be valid.

It is painful to read these circumlocutions today. We have no land ethic yet, but we have at least drawn nearer the point of admitting that birds should continue as a matter of biotic right, regardless of the presence or absence of economic advantage to us.

A parallel situation exists in respect of predatory mammals, raptorial birds, and fish-eating birds. Time was when biologists somewhat overworked the evidence that these creatures preserve the health of game by killing weaklings, or that they control rodents for the farmer, or that they prey only on 'worthless' species. Here again, the evidence had to be economic in order to be valid. It is only in recent years that we hear the more honest argument that predators are members of the community, and that no special interest has the right to exterminate them for the sake of a benefit, real or fancied, to itself. Unfortunately this enlightened view is still in the talk stage. In the field the extermination of predators goes merrily on: witness the impending erasure of the timber wolf by fiat of Congress, the Conservation Bureaus, and many state legislatures.

Some species of trees have been 'read out of the

party' by economics-minded foresters because they grow too slowly, or have too low a sale value to pay as timber crops: white cedar, tamarack, cypress, beech, and hemlock are examples. In Europe, where forestry is ecologically more advanced, the non-commercial tree species are recognized as members of the native forest community, to be preserved as such, within reason. Moreover some (like beech) have been found to have a valuable function in building up soil fertility. The interdependence of the forest and its constituent tree species, ground flora, and fauna is taken for granted.

Lack of economic value is sometimes a character not only of species or groups, but of entire biotic communities: marshes, bogs, dunes, and 'deserts' are examples. Our formula in such cases is to relegate their conservation to government as refuges, monuments, or parks. The difficulty is that these communities are usually interspersed with more valuable private lands; the government cannot possibly own or control such scattered parcels. The net effect is that we have relegated some of them to ultimate extinction over large areas. If the private owner were ecologically minded, he would be proud to be the custodian of a reasonable proportion of such areas, which add diversity and beauty to his farm and to his community.

In some instances, the assumed lack of profit in these 'waste' areas has proved to be wrong, but only after most of them had been done away with. The present scramble to reflood muskrat marshes is a case in point.

There is a clear tendency in American conservation

to relegate to government all necessary jobs that private landowners fail to perform. Government ownership, operation, subsidy, or regulation is now widely prevalent in forestry, range management, soil and watershed management, park and wilderness conservation, fisheries management, and migratory bird management, with more to come. Most of this growth in governmental conservation is proper and logical, some of it is inevitable. That I imply no disapproval of it is implicit in the fact that I have spent most of my life working for it. Nevertheless the question arises: What is the ultimate magnitude of the enterprise? Will the tax base carry its eventual ramifications? At what point will governmental conservation, like the mastodon, become handicapped by its own dimensions? The answer, if there is any, seems to be in a land ethic, or some other force which assigns more obligation to the private landowner.

Industrial landowners and users, especially lumbermen and stockmen, are inclined to wail long and loudly about the extension of government ownership and regulation to land, but (with notable exceptions) they show little disposition to develop the only visible alternative: the voluntary practice of conservation on their own lands.

When the private landowner is asked to perform some unprofitable act for the good of the community, he today assents only with outstretched palm. If the act costs him cash this is fair and proper, but when it costs only fore-thought, open-mindedness, or time, the issue is at least debatable. The overwhelming growth of land-use subsidies in recent years must be ascribed, in large part, to the government's own agencies for conservation education: the land bureaus, the agricultural colleges, and the extension services. As far as I can detect, no ethical obligation toward land is taught in these institutions.

To sum up: a system of conservation based solely on economic self-interest is hopelessly lopsided. It tends to ignore, and thus eventually to eliminate, many elements in the land community that lack commercial value, but that are (as far as we know) essential to its healthy functioning. It assumes, falsely, I think, that the economic parts of the biotic clock will function without the uneconomic parts. It tends to relegate to government many functions eventually too large, too complex, or too widely dispersed to be performed by government.

An ethical obligation on the part of the private owner is the only visible remedy for these situations.

The Land Pyramid

An ethic to supplement and guide the economic relation to land presupposes the existence of some mental image of land as a biotic mechanism. We can be ethical only in relation to something we can see, feel, understand, love, or otherwise have faith in.

The image commonly employed in conservation education is 'the balance of nature.' For reasons too lengthy to detail here, this figure of speech fails to describe accurately what little we know about the land mechanism. A much truer image is the one employed in ecology: the biotic pyramid. I shall first sketch the pyramid as a symbol of land, and later develop some of its implications in terms of land-use.

Plants absorb energy from the sun. This energy flows through a circuit called the biota, which may be represented by a pyramid consisting of layers. The bottom layer is the soil. A plant layer rests on the soil, an insect layer on the plants, a bird and rodent layer on the insects, and so on up through various animal groups to the apex layer, which consists of the larger carnivores.

The species of a layer are alike not in where they came from, or in what they look like, but rather in what they eat. Each successive layer depends on those below it for food and often for other services, and each in turn furnishes food and services to those above. Proceeding upward, each successive layer decreases in numerical abundance. Thus, for every carnivore there are hundreds of his prey, thousands of their prey, millions of insects, uncountable plants. The pyramidal form of the system reflects this numerical progression from apex to base. Man shares an intermediate layer with the bears, raccoons, and squirrels which eat both meat and vegetables.

The lines of dependency for food and other services are called food chains. Thus soil-oak-deer-Indian is a chain that has now been largely converted to soil-corn-cow-farmer. Each species, including ourselves, is a link in many chains. The deer eats a hundred plants other than oak, and the cow a hundred plants other than corn. Both, then, are links in a hundred chains. The pyramid is a tangle of chains so complex as to seem disorderly, yet the stability of the system proves it to be a highly organized structure.

Its functioning depends on the co-operation and competition of its diverse parts.

In the beginning, the pyramid of life was low and squat; the food chains short and simple. Evolution has added layer after layer, link after link. Man is one of thousands of accretions to the height and complexity of the pyramid. Science has given us many doubts, but it has given us at least one certainty: the trend of evolution is to elaborate and diversify the biota.

Land, then, is not merely soil; it is a fountain of energy flowing through a circuit of soils, plants, and animals. Food chains are the living channels which conduct energy upward; death and decay return it to the soil. The circuit is not closed; some energy is dissipated in decay, some is added by absorption from the air, some is stored in soils, peats, and long-lived forests; but it is a sustained circuit, like a slowly augmented revolving fund of life. There is always a net loss by downhill wash, but this is normally small and offset by the decay of rocks. It is deposited in the ocean and, in the course of geological time, raised to form new lands and new pyramids.

The velocity and character of the upward flow of energy depend on the complex structure of the plant and animal community, much as the upward flow of sap in a tree depends on its complex cellular organization. Without this complexity, normal circulation would presumably not occur. Structure means the characteristic numbers, as well as the characteristic kinds and functions, of the component species. This interdependence between the complex structure of the land and its smooth functioning as an energy unit is one of its basic attributes.

When a change occurs in one part of the circuit, many other parts must adjust themselves to it. Change does not necessarily obstruct or divert the flow of energy; evolution is a long series of self-induced changes, the net result of which has been to elaborate the flow mechanism and to lengthen the circuit. Evolutionary changes, however, are usually slow and local. Man's invention of tools has enabled him to make changes of unprecedented violence, rapidity, and scope.

One change is in the composition of floras and faunas. The larger predators are lopped off the apex of the pyramid; food chains, for the first time in history, become shorter rather than longer. Domesticated species from other lands are substituted for wild ones, and wild ones are moved to new habitats. In this world-wide pooling of faunas and floras, some species get out of bounds as pests and diseases, others are extinguished. Such effects are seldom intended or foreseen; they represent unpredicted and often untraceable readjustments in the structure. Agricultural science is largely a race between the emergence of new pests and the emergence of new techniques for their control.

Another change touches the flow of energy through plants and animals and its return to the soil. Fertility is the ability of soil to receive, store, and release energy. Agriculture, by overdrafts on the soil, or by too radical a substitution of domestic for native species in the superstructure, may derange the channels of flow or deplete storage. Soils depleted of their storage, or of the organic matter which anchors it, wash away faster than they form. This is erosion.

Waters, like soil, are part of the energy circuit. Industry, by polluting waters or obstructing them with dams, may exclude the plants and animals necessary to keep energy in circulation.

Transportation brings about another basic change: the plants or animals grown in one region are now consumed and returned to the soil in another. Transportation taps the energy stored in rocks, and in the air, and uses it elsewhere; thus we fertilize the garden with nitrogen gleaned by the guano birds from the fishes of seas on the other side of the Equator. Thus the formerly localized and self-contained circuits are pooled on a world-wide scale.

The process of altering the pyramid for human occupation releases stored energy, and this often gives rise, during the pioneering period, to a deceptive exuberance of plant and animal life, both wild and tame. These releases of biotic capital tend to becloud or postpone the penalties of violence.

*   *   *

This thumbnail sketch of land as an energy circuit conveys three basic ideas:

(1) That land is not merely soil.

(2) That the native plants and animals kept the energy circuit open; others may or may not.

(3) That man-made changes are of a different order than evolutionary changes, and have effects more comprehensive than is intended or foreseen.

These ideas, collectively, raise two basic issues: Can the land adjust itself to the new order? Can the desired alterations be accomplished with less violence?

Biotas seem to differ in their capacity to sustain violent conversion. Western Europe, for example, carries a far different pyramid than Caesar found there. Some large animals are lost; swampy forests have become meadows or plowland; many new plants and animals are introduced, some of which escape as pests; the remaining natives are greatly changed in distribution and abundance. Yet the soil is still there and, with the help of imported nutrients, still fertile; the waters flow normally; the new structure seems to function and to persist. There is no visible stoppage or derangement of the circuit.

Western Europe, then, has a resistant biota. Its inner processes are tough, elastic, resistant to strain. No matter how violent the alterations, the pyramid, so far, has developed some new *modus vivendi* which preserves its habitability for man, and for most of the other natives.

Japan seems to present another instance of radical conversion without disorganization.

Most other civilized regions, and some as yet barely touched by civilization, display various stages of disorganization, varying from initial symptoms to advanced wastage. In Asia Minor and North Africa diagnosis is confused by climatic changes, which may have been either the cause or the effect of advanced wastage. In the United States the degree of disorganization varies locally; it is worst in the Southwest, the Ozarks, and parts of the South, and least in New England and the Northwest. Better land-uses may still arrest it in the less advanced regions. In parts of

Mexico, South America, South Africa, and Australia a violent and accelerating wastage is in progress, but I cannot assess the prospects.

This almost world-wide display of disorganization in the land seems to be similar to disease in an animal, except that it never culminates in complete disorganization or death. The land recovers, but at some reduced level of complexity, and with a reduced carrying capacity for people, plants, and animals. Many biotas currently regarded as 'lands of opportunity' are in fact already subsisting on exploitative agriculture, i.e. they have already exceeded their sustained carrying capacity. Most of South America is overpopulated in this sense.

In arid regions we attempt to offset the process of wastage by reclamation, but it is only too evident that the prospective longevity of reclamation projects is often short. In our own West, the best of them may not last a century.

The combined evidence of history and ecology seems to support one general deduction: the less violent the man-made changes, the greater the probability of successful readjustment in the pyramid. Violence, in turn, varies with human population density; a dense population requires a more violent conversion. In this respect, North America has a better chance for permanence than Europe, if she can contrive to limit her density.

This deduction runs counter to our current philosophy, which assumes that because a small increase in density enriched human life, that an indefinite increase will enrich it indefinitely. Ecology knows of no density relationship that holds for indefinitely wide limits. All gains from density are subject to a law of diminishing returns.

Whatever may be the equation for men and land, it is improbable that we as yet know all its terms. Recent discoveries in mineral and vitamin nutrition reveal unsuspected dependencies in the up-circuit: incredibly minute quantities of certain substances determine the value of soils to plants, of plants to animals. What of the down-circuit? What of the vanishing species, the preservation of which we now regard as an esthetic luxury? They helped build the soil; in what unsuspected ways may they be essential to its maintenance? Professor Weaver proposes that we use prairie flowers to reflocculate the wasting soils of the dust bowl; who knows for what purpose cranes and condors, otters and grizzlies may some day be used?

Land Health and the A-B Cleavage

A land, ethic, then, reflects the existence of an ecological conscience, and this in turn reflects a conviction of individual responsibility for the health of the land. Health is the capacity of the land for self-renewal. Conservation is our effort to understand and preserve this capacity.

Conservationists are notorious for their dissensions. Superficially these seem to add up to mere confusion, but a more careful scrutiny reveals a single plane of cleavage common to many specialized fields. In each field one group (A) regards the land as soil, and its function as commodity-production; another group (B) regards the land as a biota, and its function as something broader. How much broader is admittedly in a state of doubt and confusion.

In my own field, forestry, group A is quite content to grow trees like cabbages, with cellulose as the basic forest commodity. It feels no inhibition against violence; its ideology is agronomic. Group B, on the other hand, sees forestry as fundamentally different from agronomy because it employs natural species, and manages a natural environment rather than creating an artificial one. Group B prefers natural reproduction on principle. It worries on biotic as well as economic grounds about the loss of species like chestnut, and the threatened loss of the white pines. It worries about a whole series of secondary forest functions: wildlife, recreation, watersheds, wilderness areas. To my mind, Group B feels the stirrings of an ecological conscience.

In the wildlife field, a parallel cleavage exists. For Group A the basic commodities are sport and meat; the yardsticks of production are ciphers of take in pheasants and trout. Artificial propagation is acceptable as a permanent as well as a temporary recourse— if its unit costs permit. Group B, on the other hand, worries about a whole series of biotic side-issues. What is the cost in predators of producing a game crop? Should we have further recourse to exotics? How can management restore the shrinking species, like prairie grouse, already hopeless as shootable game? How can management restore the threatened rarities, like trumpeter swan and whooping crane? Can management principles be extended to wildflowers? Here again it is clear to me that we have the same A-B cleavage as in forestry.

In the larger field of agriculture I am less competent to speak, but there seem to be somewhat parallel cleavages. Scientific agriculture was actively developing before ecology was born, hence a slower penetration of ecological concepts might be expected. Moreover the farmer, by the very nature of his techniques, must modify the biota more radically than the forester or the wildlife manager. Nevertheless, there are many discontents in agriculture which seem to add up to a new vision of 'biotic farming.'

Perhaps the most important of these is the new evidence that poundage or tonnage is no measure of the food-value of farm crops; the products of fertile soil may be qualitatively as well as quantitatively superior. We can bolster poundage from depleted soils by pouring on imported fertility, but we are not necessarily bolstering food-value. The possible ultimate ramifications of this idea are so immense that I must leave their exposition to abler pens.

The discontent that labels itself 'organic farming,' while bearing some of the earmarks of a cult, is nevertheless biotic in its direction, particularly in its insistence on the importance of soil flora and fauna.

The ecological fundamentals of agriculture are just as poorly known to the public as in other fields of land-use. For example, few educated people realize that the marvelous advances in technique made during recent decades are improvements in the pump, rather than the well. Acre for acre, they have barely sufficed to offset the sinking level of fertility.

In all of these cleavages, we see repeated the same basic paradoxes: man the conqueror *versus* man the biotic citizen; science the sharpener of his sword *versus* science the searchlight on his universe; land the slave and servant *versus* land the collective organism. Robinson's injunction to Tristram may well be applied, at this juncture, to *Homo sapiens* as a species in geological time:

> Whether you will or not
> You are a King, Tristram, for you are one
> Of the time-tested few that leave the world,
> When they are gone, not the same place it was.
> Mark what you leave.

The Outlook

It is inconceivable to me that an ethical relation to land can exist without love, respect, and admiration for land, and a high regard for its value. By value, I of course men something far broader than mere economic value; I mean value in the philosophical sense.

Perhaps the most serious obstacle impeding the evolution of a land ethic is the fact that our educational and economic system is headed away from, rather than toward, an intense consciousness of land. Your true modern is separated from the land by many middlemen, and by innumerable physical gadgets. He has no vital relation to it; to him it is the space between cities on which crops grow. Turn him loose for a day on the land, and if the spot does not happen to be a golf links or a 'scenic' area, he is bored stiff. If crops could be raised by hydroponics instead of farming, it would suit him very well. Synthetic substitutes for wood, leather, wool, and other

natural land products suit him better than the origi-
nals. In short, land is something he has 'outgrown.'

Almost equally serious as an obstacle to a land ethic
is the attitude of the farmer for whom the land is
still an adversary, or a taskmaster that keeps him in
slavery. Theoretically, the mechanization of farming
ought to cut the farmer's chains, but whether it really
does is debatable.

One of the requisites for an ecological comprehension of land is an understanding of ecology, and this
is by no means co-extensive with 'education'; in fact,
much higher education seems deliberately to avoid
ecological concepts. An understanding of ecology
does not necessarily originate in courses bearing ecological labels; it is quite as likely to be labeled geography, botany, agronomy, history, or economics. This
is as it should be, but whatever the label, ecological
training is scarce.

The case for a land ethic would appear hopeless
but for the minority which is in obvious revolt
against these 'modern' trends.

The 'key-log' which must be moved to release the
evolutionary process for an ethic is simply this: quit
thinking about decent land-use as solely an economic
problem. Examine each question in terms of what is
ethically and esthetically right, as well as what is eco-
nomically expedient. A thing is right when it tends
to preserve the integrity, stability, and beauty of the
biotic community. It is wrong when it tends otherwise.

It of course goes without saying that economic
feasibility limits the tether of what can or cannot be
done for land. It always has and it always will. The
fallacy the economic determinists have tied around

our collective neck, and which we now need to cast
off, is the belief that economics determines *all* land-
use. This is simply not true. An innumerable host of
actions and attitudes, comprising perhaps the bulk of
all land relations, is determined by the land-users'
tastes and predilections, rather than by his purse.
The bulk of all land relations hinges on investments
of time, forethought, skill, and faith rather than on
investments of cash. As a land-user thinketh, so is he.

I have purposely presented the land ethic as a
product of social evolution because nothing so important as an ethic is ever 'written.' Only the most
superficial student of history supposes that Moses
'wrote' the Decalogue; it evolved in the minds of a
thinking community, and Moses wrote a tentative summary of it for a 'seminar.' I say tentative because
evolution never stops.

The evolution of a land ethic is an intellectual as
well as emotional process. Conservation is paved with
good intentions which prove to be futile, or even
dangerous, because they are devoid of critical understanding either of the land, or of economic land-use.
I think it is a truism that as the ethical frontier advances from the individual to the community, its intellectual content increases.

The mechanism of operation is the same for any
ethic: social approbation for right actions: social disapproval for wrong actions.

By and large, our present problem is one of attitudes and implements. We are remodeling the Al-
hambra with a steam-shovel, and we are proud of
our yardage. We shall hardly relinquish the shovel,
which after all has many good points, but we are in

need of gentler and more objective criteria for its successful use.

Wilderness

WILDERNESS IS the raw material out of which man has hammered the artifact called civilization.

Wilderness was never a homogeneous raw material. It was very diverse, and the resulting artifacts are very diverse. These differences in the end-product are known as cultures. The rich diversity of the world's cultures reflects a corresponding diversity in the wilds that gave them birth.

For the first time in the history of the human species, two changes are now impending. One is the exhaustion of wilderness in the more habitable portions of the globe. The other is the world-wide hybridization of cultures through modern transport and industrialization. Neither can be prevented, and perhaps should not be, but the question arises whether, by some slight amelioration of the impending changes, certain values can be preserved that would otherwise be lost.

To the laborer in the sweat of his labor, the raw stuff on his anvil is an adversary to be conquered. So was wilderness an adversary to the pioneer.

But to the laborer in repose, able for the moment to cast a philosophical eye on his world, that same raw stuff is something to be loved and cherished, because it gives definition and meaning to his life. This is a plea for the preservation of some tag-ends of wilderness, as museum pieces, for the edification of those who may one day wish to see, feel, or study the origins of their cultural inheritance.

The Remnants

Many of the diverse wildernesses out of which we have hammered America are already gone; hence in any practical program the unit areas to be preserved must vary greatly in size and in degree of wildness.

No living man will see again the long-grass prairie, where a sea of prairie flowers lapped at the stirrups of the pioneer. We shall do well to find a forty here and there on which the prairie plants can be kept alive as species. There were a hundred such plants, many of exceptional beauty. Most of them are quite unknown to those who have inherited their domain.

But the short-grass prairie, where Cabeza de Vaca saw the horizon under the bellies of the buffalo, is still extant in a few spots of 10,000-acre size, albeit severely chewed up by sheep, cattle, and dry-farmers. If the forty-niners are worth commemorating on the walls of state capitols, is not the scene of their mighty hegira worth commemorating in several national prairie reservations?

No living man will see again the virgin pineries of the Lake States, or the flatwoods of the coastal plain, or the giant hardwoods; of these, samples of a few acres each will have to suffice. But there are still sev-

eral blocks of maple-hemlock of thousand-acre size;
there are similar blocks of Appalachian hardwoods,
of southern hardwood swamp, of cypress swamp, and
of Adirondack spruce. Few of these tag-ends are secure from prospective cuttings, and fewer still from
prospective tourist roads.

One of the fastest-shrinking categories of wilderness is coastlines. Cottages and tourist roads have all
but annihilated wild coasts on both oceans, and Lake
Superior is now losing the last large remnant of wild

shoreline on the Great Lakes. No single kind of wilderness is more intimately interwoven with history, and none nearer the point of complete disappearance.

In all of North America east of the Rockies, there is only one large area formally reserved as a wilderness: the Quetico-Superior International Park in Minnesota and Ontario. This magnificent block of canoe-country, a mosaic of lakes and rivers, lies mostly in Canada, and can be about as large as Canada chooses to make it, but its integrity is threatened by two recent developments: the growth of fishing resorts served by pontoon-equipped airplanes, and a jurisdictional dispute whether the Minnesota end of the area shall be all National Forest, or partly State Forest. The whole region is in danger of power impoundments, and this regrettable cleavage among proponents of wilderness may end in giving power the whiphand.

In the Rocky Mountain states, a score of areas in the National Forests, varying in size from a hundred thousand to half a million acres, are withdrawn as wilderness, and closed to roads, hotels, and other inimical uses. In the National Parks the same principle is recognized, but no specific boundaries are delimited. Collectively, these federal areas are the backbone of the wilderness program, but they are not so secure as the paper record might lead one to believe. Local pressures for new tourist roads knock off a chip here and a slab there. There is perennial pressure for extension of roads for forest-fire control, and these, by slow degrees, become public highways. Idle CCC camps presented a widespread temptation to build new and often needless roads. Lumber shortages during the war gave the impetus of military necessity to many road extensions, legitimate and otherwise. At the present moment, ski-tows and ski-hotels are being promoted in many mountain areas, often without regard to their prior designation as wilderness.

One of the most insidious invasions of wilderness is via predator control. It works thus: wolves and lions are cleaned out of a wilderness area in the interest of big-game management. The big-game herds (usually deer or elk) then increase to the point of overbrowsing the range. Hunters must then be encouraged to harvest the surplus, but modern hunters refuse to operate far from a car; hence a road must be built to provide access to the surplus game. Again and again, wilderness areas have been split by this process, but it still continues.

The Rocky Mountain system of wilderness areas covers a wide gamut of forest types, from the juniper breaks of the Southwest to the 'illimitable woods where rolls the Oregon.' It is lacking, however, in desert areas, probably because of that under-aged brand of esthetics which limits the definition of 'scenery' to lakes and pine trees.

In Canada and Alaska there are still large expanses of virgin country

Where nameless men by nameless rivers wander
and in strange valleys die strange deaths alone.

A representative series of these areas can, and should, be kept. Many are of negligible or negative value for economic use. It will be contended, of course, that no deliberate planning to this end is necessary; that adequate areas will survive anyhow.

All recent history belies so comforting an assumption. Even if wild spots do survive, what of their fauna? The woodland caribou, the several races of mountain sheep, the pure form of woods buffalo, the barren ground grizzly, the freshwater seals, and the whales are even now threatened. Of what use are wild areas destitute of their distinctive faunas? There are now organizations and development groups actively embarked on the industrialization of the Arctic wastes, and plans even larger are actively being pressed. The wilderness of the Far North as yet has no formal protection and though still extensive, is beginning to dwindle.

To what extent Canada and Alaska will be able to see and grasp their opportunities is anybody's guess. Pioneers usually scoff at any effort to perpetuate pioneering.

Wilderness for Recreation

Physical combat for the means of subsistence was, for unnumbered centuries, an economic fact. When it disappeared as such, a sound instinct led us to preserve it in the form of athletic sports and games.

Physical combat between men and beasts was, in like manner, an economic fact, now preserved as hunting and fishing for sport.

Public wilderness areas are, first of all, a means of perpetuating, in sport form, the more virile and primitive skills in pioneering travel and subsistence.

Some of these skills are of generalized distribution; the details have been adapted to the American scene, but the skill is world-wide. Hunting, fishing, and foot travel by pack are examples.

Two of them, however, are as American as a hickory tree; they have been copied elsewhere, but they were developed to their full perfection only on this continent. One of these is canoe travel, and the other is travel by pack-train. Both are shrinking rapidly. Your Hudson Bay Indian now has a put-put, and your mountaineer a Ford. If I had to make a living by canoe or packhorse, I should likely do likewise, for both are grueling labor. But we who seek wilderness travel for sport are foiled when we are forced to

compete with mechanized substitutes. It is bootless to execute a portage to the tune of motor launches, or to turn out your bell-mare in the pasture of a summer hotel. It is better to stay home.

Wilderness areas are first of all a series of sanctuaries for the primitive arts of wilderness travel, especially canoeing and packing.

I suppose some will wish to debate whether it is important to keep these primitive arts alive. I shall not debate it. Either you know it in your bones, or you are very, very old.

European hunting and fishing are largely devoid of the thing that wilderness areas might be the means of preserving in this country. Europeans do not camp, cook, or do their own work in the woods if they can avoid doing so. Work chores are delegated to beaters and servants, and a hunt carries the atmosphere of a picnic, rather than of pioneering. The test of skill is confined largely to the actual taking of game or fish.

There are those who decry wilderness sports as 'undemocratic' because the recreational carrying capacity of a wilderness is small, as compared with a golf links or a tourist camp. The basic error in such argument is that it applies the philosophy of mass-production to what is intended to counteract mass-production. The value of recreation is not a matter of ciphers. Recreation is valuable in proportion to the intensity of its experiences, and to the degree to which it *differs from* and *contrasts with* workaday life. By these criteria, mechanized outings are at best a milk-and-water affair.

Mechanized recreation already has seized nine-tenths of the woods and mountains; a decent respect for minorities should dedicate the other tenth to wilderness.

Wilderness for Science

The most important characteristic of an organism is that capacity for internal self-renewal known as health.

There are two organisms whose processes of self-renewal have been subjected to human interference and control. One of these is man himself (medicine and public health). The other is land (agriculture and conservation).

The effort to control the health of land has not been very successful. It is now generally understood that when soil loses fertility, or washes away faster than it forms, and when water systems exhibit abnormal floods and shortages, the land is sick.

Other derangements are known as facts, but are not yet thought of as symptoms of land sickness. The disappearance of plants and animal species without visible cause, despite efforts to protect them, and the irruption of others as pests despite efforts to control them, must, in the absence of simpler explanations, be regarded as symptoms of sickness in the land organism. Both are occurring too frequently to be dismissed as normal evolutionary events.

The status of thought on these ailments of the land is reflected in the fact that our treatments for them are still prevailingly local. Thus when a soil loses fertility we pour on fertilizer, or at best alter its tame flora and fauna, without considering the fact that its wild flora and fauna, which built the soil to begin with, may likewise be important to its maintenance. It was recently discovered, for example, that good tobacco crops depend, for some unknown reason, on the preconditioning of the soil by wild ragweed. It does not occur to us that such unexpected chains of dependency may have wide prevalence in nature.

When prairie dogs, ground squirrels, or mice increase to pest levels we poison them, but we do not look beyond the animal to find the cause of the irruption. We assume that animal troubles must have animal causes. The latest scientific evidence points to derangements of the *plant* community as the real seat of rodent irruptions, but few explorations of this clue are being made.

Many forest plantations are producing one-log or two-log trees on soil which originally grew three-log and four-log trees. Why? Thinking foresters know that the cause probably lies not in the tree, but in the micro-flora of the soil, and that it may take more years to restore the soil flora than it took to destroy it.

Many conservation treatments are obviously superficial. Flood-control dams have no relation to the cause of floods. Check dams and terraces do not touch the cause of erosion. Refuges and hatcheries to maintain the supply of game and fish do not explain why the supply fails to maintain itself.

In general, the trend of the evidence indicates that in land, just as in the human body, the symptoms may lie in one organ and the cause in another. The practices we now call conservation are, to a large extent, local alleviations of biotic pain. They are necessary, but they must not be confused with cures. The art of land doctoring is being practiced with vigor, but the science of land health is yet to be born.

A science of land health needs, first of all, a base datum of normality, a picture of how healthy land maintains itself as an organism.

We have two available norms. One is found where land physiology remains largely normal despite centuries of human occupation. I know of only one such place: northeastern Europe. It is not likely that we shall fail to study it.

The other and most perfect norm is wilderness. Paleontology offers abundant evidence that wilderness maintained itself for immensely long periods; that its component species were rarely lost, neither did they get out of hand; that weather and water built soil as fast or faster than it was carried away. Wilderness, then, assumes unexpected importance as a laboratory for the study of land-health.

One cannot study the physiology of Montana in

the Amazon; each biotic province needs its own wilderness for comparative studies of used and unused land. It is of course too late to salvage more than a lopsided system of wilderness study areas, and most of these remnants are far too small to retain their normality in all respects. Even the National Parks, which run up to a million acres each in size, have not been large enough to retain their natural predators, or to exclude animal diseases carried by livestock. Thus the Yellowstone has lost its wolves and cougars, with the result that elk are ruining the flora, particularly on the winter range. At the same time the grizzly bear and the mountain sheep are shrinking, the latter by reason of disease.

While even the largest wilderness areas become partially deranged, it required only a few wild acres for J. E. Weaver to discover why the prairie flora is more drouth-resistant than the agronomic flora which has supplanted it. Weaver found that the prairie species practice 'team work' underground by distributing their root-systems to cover all levels, whereas the species comprising the agronomic rotation overdraw one level and neglect another, thus building up cumulative deficits. An important agronomic principle emerged from Weaver's researches.

Again, it required only a few wild acres for Togrediak to discover why pines on old fields never achieve the size or wind-firmness of pines on uncleared forest soils. In the latter case, the roots follow old root channels, and thus strike deeper.

In many cases we literally do not know how good a performance to expect of healthy land unless we have a wild area for comparison with sick ones. Thus most of the early travelers in the Southwest describe the mountain rivers as originally clear, but a doubt remains, for they may, by accident, have seen them at favorable seasons. Erosion engineers had no base datum until it was discovered that exactly similar rivers in the Sierra Madre of Chihuahua, never grazed or used for fear of Indians, show at their worst a milky hue, not too cloudy for a trout fly. Moss grows to the water's edge on their banks. Most of the corresponding rivers in Arizona and New Mexico are ribbons of boulders, mossless, soil-less, and all but treeless. The preservation and study of the Sierra Madre wilderness by an international experiment station, as a norm for the cure of sick land on both sides of the border, would be a good-neighbor enterprise well worthy of consideration.

In short all available wild areas, large or small, are likely to have value as norms for land science. Recreation is not their only, or even their principal, utility.

Wilderness for Wildlife

The National Parks do not suffice as a means of perpetuating the larger carnivores; witness the precarious status of the grizzly bear, and the fact that the park system is already wolfless. Neither do they suffice for mountain sheep; most sheep herds are shrinking.

The reasons for this are clear in some cases and obscure in others. The parks are certainly too small for such a far-ranging species as the wolf. Many animal species, for reasons unknown, do not seem to thrive as detached islands of population.

The most feasible way to enlarge the area available for wilderness fauna is for the wilder parts of the National Forests, which usually surround the Parks, to function as parks in respect to threatened species. That they have not so functioned is tragically illustrated in the case of the grizzly bear.

In 1909, when I first saw the West, there were grizzlies in every major mountain mass, but you could travel for months without meeting a conservation officer. Today there is some kind of conservation officer 'behind every bush,' yet as wildlife bureaus grow, our most magnificent mammal retreats steadily toward the Canadian border. Of the 6000 grizzlies officially reported as remaining in areas owned by the United States, 5000 are in Alaska. Only five states have any at all. There seems to be a tacit assumption that if grizzlies survive in Canada and Alaska, that is good enough. It is not good enough for me. The Alaskan bears are a distinct species. Relegating grizzlies to Alaska is about like relegating happiness to heaven; one may never get there.

Saving the grizzly requires a series of large areas from which roads and livestock are excluded, or in which livestock damage is compensated. Buying out scattered livestock ranches is the only way to create such areas, but despite large authority to buy and exchange lands, the conservation bureaus have accomplished virtually nothing toward this end. The Forest Service has established a grizzly range in Montana, but I know of a mountain range in Utah in which the Forest Service actually promoted a sheep industry, despite the fact that it harbored the sole remnant of grizzlies in that state.

Permanent grizzly ranges and permanent wilderness areas are of course two names for one problem. Enthusiasm about either requires a long view of conservation, and a historical perspective. Only those able to see the pageant of evolution can be expected to value its theater, the wilderness, or its outstanding achievement, the grizzly. But if education really educates, there will, in time, be more and more citizens who understand that relics of the old West add meaning and value to the new. Youth yet unborn will pole up the Missouri with Lewis and Clark, or climb the Sierras with James Capen Adams, and each generation in turn will ask: Where is the big white bear? It will be a sorry answer to say he went under while conservationists weren't looking.

Defenders of Wilderness

Wilderness is a resource which can shrink but not grow. Invasions can be arrested or modified in a manner to keep an area usable either for recreation, or for science, or for wildlife, but the creation of new wilderness in the full sense of the word is impossible.

It follows, then, that any wilderness program is a rearguard action, through which retreats are reduced to a minimum. The Wilderness Society was organized in 1935 'for the one purpose of saving the wilderness remnants in America.' The Sierra Club is doing yeoman work toward the same end.

It does not suffice, however, to have a few such

societies, nor can one be content that Congress has enacted a bill aimed at wilderness preservation. Unless there be wilderness-minded men scattered through all the conservation bureaus, the societies may never learn of new invasions until the time for action has passed. Furthermore, a militant minority of wilderness-minded citizens must be on watch throughout the nation and vigilantly available for action.

In Europe, where wilderness has now retreated to the Carpathians and Siberia, every thinking conservationist bemoans its loss. Even in Britain, which has less room for land-luxuries than almost any other civilized country, there is a vigorous if belated movement for saving a few small spots of semi-wild land.

Ability to see the cultural value of wilderness boils down, in the last analysis, to a question of intellectual humility. The shallow-minded modern who has lost his rootage in the land assumes that he has already discovered what is important; it is such who prate of empires, political or economic, that will last a thousand years. It is only the scholar who appreciates that all history consists of successive excursions from a single starting-point, to which man returns again and again to organize yet another search for a durable scale of values. It is only the scholar who understands why the raw wilderness gives definition and meaning to the human enterprise.

Conservation Esthetic

BARRING LOVE and war, few enterprises are undertaken with such abandon, or by such diverse individuals, or with so paradoxical a mixture of appetite and altruism, as that group of avocations known as outdoor recreation. It is, by common consent, a good thing for people to get back to nature. But wherein lies the goodness, and what can be done to encourage its pursuit? On these questions there is confusion of counsel, and only the most uncritical minds are free from doubt.

Recreation became a problem with a name in the days of the elder Roosevelt, when the railroads which had banished the countryside from the city began to carry city-dwellers, *en masse*, to the countryside. It began to be noticed that the greater the exodus, the smaller the per-capita ration of peace, solitude, wildlife, and scenery, and the longer the migration to reach them.

The automobile has spread this once mild and local predicament to the outermost limits of good roads —it has made scarce in the hinterlands something once abundant on the back forty. But that something must nevertheless be found. Like ions shot from the sun, the week-enders radiate from every town, generating heat and friction as they go. A tourist industry purveys bed and board to bait more ions, faster, further. Advertisements on rock and rill confide to all and sundry the whereabouts of new retreats, landscapes, hunting-grounds, and fishing-lakes just beyond those recently overrun. Bureaus build roads into new hinterlands, then buy more hinterlands to absorb the exodus accelerated by the roads. A gadget industry pads the bumps against nature-in-the-raw; woodcraft becomes the art of using gadgets. And now, to cap the pyramid of banalities, the trailer. To him who seeks in the woods and mountains only those things obtainable from travel or golf, the present situation is tolerable. But to him who seeks something more, recreation has become a self-destructive process of seeking but never quite finding, a major frustration of mechanized society.

The retreat of the wilderness under the barrage of motorized tourists is no local thing; Hudson Bay, Alaska, Mexico, South Africa are giving way, and South America and Siberia are next. Drums along the Mohawk are now honks along the rivers of the world. *Homo sapiens* putters no more under his own vine and fig tree; he has poured into his gas tank the stored motivity of countless creatures aspiring through the ages to wiggle their way to pastures new. Antlike he swarms the continents.

This is Outdoor Recreation, Latest Model.

Who now is the recreationist, and what does he seek? A few samples will remind us.

Take a look, first, at any duck marsh. A cordon of
parked cars surrounds it. Crouched on each point of
its reedy margin is some pillar of society, automatic
ready, trigger finger itching to break, if need be,
every law of commonwealth or commonweal to kill
a duck. That he is already overfed in no way damp-
ens his avidity for gathering his meat from God.

Wandering in the near-by woods is another pillar,
hunting rare ferns or new warblers. Because his kind
of hunting seldom calls for theft or pillage, he disdains the killer. Yet, like as not, in his youth he was
one.

At some near-by resort is still another nature-lover
—the kind who writes bad verse on birchbark. Everywhere is the unspecialized motorist whose recreation
is mileage, who has run the gamut of the National
Parks in one summer, and now is headed for Mexico
City and points south.

Lastly, there is the professional, striving through
countless conservation organizations to give the
nature-seeking public what it wants, or to make it
want what he has to give.

Why, it may be asked, should such a diversity of
folk be bracketed in a single category? Because each,
in his own way, is a hunter. And why does each call
himself a conservationist? Because the wild things he
hunts for have eluded his grasp, and he hopes by
some necromancy of laws, appropriations, regional
plans, reorganization of departments, or other form
of mass-wishing to make them stay put.

Recreation is commonly spoken of as an economic
resource. Senate committees tell us, in reverent ci-

phers, how many millions the public spends in its pursuit. It has indeed an economic aspect—a cottage on a fishing-lake, or even a duck-point on a marsh, may cost as much as the entire adjacent farm.

It has also an ethical aspect. In the scramble for unspoiled places, codes and decalogues evolve. We hear of 'outdoor manners.' We indoctrinate youth. We print definitions of 'What is a sportsman?' and hang a copy on the wall of whosoever will pay a dollar for the propagation of the faith.

It is clear, though, that these economic and ethical manifestations are results, not causes, of the motive force. We seek contacts with nature because we derive pleasure from them. As in opera, economic machinery is employed to create and maintain facilities. As in opera, professionals make a living out of creating and maintaining them, but it would be false to say of either that the basic motive, the *raison d'être*, is economic. The duck-hunter in his blind and the operatic singer on the stage, despite the disparity of their accoutrements, are doing the same thing. Each is reviving, in play, a drama formerly inherent in daily life. Both are, in the last analysis, esthetic exercises.

Public policies for outdoor recreation are controversial. Equally conscientious citizens hold opposite views on what it is and what should be done to conserve its resource-base. Thus the Wilderness Society seeks to exclude roads from the hinterlands, and the Chamber of Commerce to extend them, both in the name of recreation. The game-farmer kills hawks and the bird-lover protects them in the name of shotgun and field-glass hunting respectively. Such factions commonly label each other with short and ugly names, when, in fact, each is considering a different component of the recreational process. These components *differ widely in their characteristics or properties*. A given policy may be true for one but false for another.

It seems timely, therefore, to segregate the components, and to examine the distinctive characteristics or properties of each.

We begin with the simplest and most obvious: the physical objects that the outdoorsman may seek, find, capture, and carry away. In this category are wild crops such as game and fish, and the symbols or tokens of achievement such as heads, hides, photographs, and specimens.

All these things rest upon the idea of *trophy*. The pleasure they give is, or should be, in the seeking as well as in the getting. The trophy, whether it be a bird's egg, a mass of trout, a basket of mushrooms, the photograph of a bear, the pressed specimen of a wild flower, or a note tucked into the cairn on a mountain peak, is a *certificate*. It attests that its owner has been somewhere and done something— that he has exercised skill, persistence, or discrimination in the age-old feat of overcoming, outwitting, or reducing-to-possession. These connotations which attach to the trophy usually far exceed its physical value.

But trophies differ in their reactions to mass-pursuit. The yield of game and fish can, by means of propagation or management, be increased so as to give each hunter more, or to give more hunters the same amount. During the past decade a profession of wildlife management has sprung into existence. A score of universities teach its techniques, conduct research for bigger and better wild animal crops. However, when carried too far, this stepping-up of yields is subject to a law of diminishing returns. Very intensive management of game or fish lowers the unit value of the trophy by artificializing it.

Consider, for example, a trout raised in a hatchery and newly liberated in an over-fished stream. The stream is no longer capable of natural trout production. Pollution has fouled its waters, or deforestation and trampling have warmed or silted them. No one would claim that this trout has the same value as a wholly wild one caught out of some unmanaged stream in the high Rockies. Its esthetic connotations are inferior, even though its capture may require skill. (Its liver, one authority says, is also so degenerated by hatchery feeding as to forebode an early death.) Yet several over-fished states now depend almost entirely on such man-made trout.

All intergrades of artificiality exist, but as mass-use increases it tends to push the whole gamut of conservation techniques toward the artificial end, and the whole scale of trophy-values downward.

To safeguard this expensive, artificial, and more or less helpless trout, the Conservation Commission feels impelled to kill all herons and terns visiting the

hatchery where it was raised, and all mergansers and otters inhabiting the stream in which it is released. The fisherman perhaps feels no loss in this sacrifice of one kind of wild life for another, but the ornithologist is ready to bite off ten-penny nails. Artificialized management has, in effect, bought fishing at the expense of another and perhaps higher recreation; it has paid dividends to one citizen out of capital stock belonging to all. The same kind of biological wildcatting prevails in game management. In Europe, where wild-crop statistics are available for long periods, we even know the 'rate of exchange' of game for predators. Thus, in Saxony one hawk is killed for each seven game birds bagged, and one predator of some kind for each three head of small game.

Damage to plant life usually follows artificialized management of animals—for example, damage to forests by deer. One may see this in north Germany, in northeast Pennsylvania, in the Kaibab, and in dozens of other less publicized regions. In each case over-abundant deer, when deprived of their natural enemies, have made it impossible for deer food plants to survive or reproduce. Beech, maple, and yew in Europe, ground hemlock and white cedar in the eastern states, mountain mahogany and cliff-rose in the West, are deer foods threatened by artificialized deer. The composition of the flora, from wild flowers to forest trees, is gradually impoverished, and the deer

in turn are dwarfed by malnutrition. There are no stags in the woods today like those whose antlers decorated the walls of feudal castles.

On the English heaths, reproduction of trees is inhibited by rabbits over-protected in the process of cropping partridges and pheasants. On scores of tropical islands both flora and fauna have been destroyed by goats introduced for meat and sport. It would be hard to calculate the mutual injuries by and between mammals deprived of their natural predators, and ranges stripped of their natural food plants. Agricultural crops caught between these upper and nether millstones of ecological mismanagement are saved only at the cost of endless indemnities and barbed wire.

We generalize, then, by saying that mass-use tends to dilute the quality of organic trophies like game and fish, and to induce damage to other resources such as non-game animals, natural vegetation, and farm crops.

The same dilution and damage is not apparent in the yield of 'indirect' trophies, such as photographs. Broadly speaking, a piece of scenery snapped by a dozen tourist cameras daily is not physically impaired thereby, nor does it suffer if photographed a hundred times. The camera industry is one of the few innocuous parasites on wild nature.

We have, then, a basic difference in reaction to mass-use as between two categories of physical objects pursued as trophies.

Let us now consider another component of recreation, which is more subtle and complex: the feeling of isolation in nature. That this is acquiring a scarcity-value that is very high to some persons is attested by the wilderness controversy. Wilderness areas are by official definition roadless, with roads built only to their edges. They are thus advertised as unique, as indeed they are. But before long trails are congested, there is pressure for access from the air; or an unexpected fire necessitates splitting an area in two with a road to haul fire-fighters. Or the congestion induced by publicity may whip up the price of guides and packers, whereupon somebody discovers that the wilderness policy is undemocratic. Or the local Chamber of Commerce, at first quiescent at the novelty of a hinterland officially labeled as 'wild,' tastes its first blood of tourist money. It then wants more, wilderness or no wilderness. The jeep and the airplane, creatures of the ever mounting pressure from humanity, thus eliminate the opportunity for isolation in nature.

In short, the very scarcity of wild places, reacting with the *mores* of advertising and promotion, tends to defeat any deliberate effort to prevent their growing still more scarce.

It is clear without further discussion that mass-use involves a direct dilution of the opportunity for solitude; that when we speak of roads, campgrounds, trails, and toilets as 'development' of recreational resources, we speak falsely in respect to this component. Such accommodations for the crowd are not developing (in the sense of adding or creating) anything. On the contrary, they are merely water poured into the already-thin soup.

We now contrast with the isolation-component that very distinct if simple one which we may label 'fresh-air and change of scene.' Mass-use neither destroys nor dilutes this value. The thousandth tourist who clicks the gate to the National Park breathes approximately the same air, and experiences the same contrast with Monday-at-the-office, as does the first. One might even believe that the gregarious assault on the outdoors enhances the contrast. We may say, then, that the fresh-air and change-of-scene component is like the photographic trophy—it withstands mass-use without damage.

We come now to another component: the perception of the natural processes by which the land and the living things upon it have achieved their characteristic forms (evolution) and by which they maintain their existence (ecology). That thing called 'nature study,' despite the shiver it brings to the spines of the elect, constitutes the first embryonic groping of the mass-mind toward perception.

The outstanding characteristic of perception is that it entails no consumption and no dilution of any resource. The swoop of a hawk, for example, is perceived by one as the drama of evolution. To another it is only a threat to the full frying-pan. The drama may excite a hundred successive witnesses, the threat only one—for he responds with a shotgun.

To promote perception is the only truly creative part of recreational engineering.

This fact is important, and its potential power for bettering 'the good life' only dimly understood. When Daniel Boone first entered into the forests and prairies of 'the dark and bloody ground,' he reduced to his possession the pure essence of 'outdoor America.' He didn't call it that, but what he found is the thing we now seek, and we here deal with things not names.

Recreation, however, is not the outdoors, but our reaction to it. Daniel Boone's reaction depended not only on the quality of what he saw, but on the quality of the mental eye with which he saw it. Ecological science has wrought a change in the mental eye. It has disclosed origins and functions for what to Boone were only facts. It has disclosed mechanisms for what to Boone were only attributes. We have no yardstick to measure this change, but we may safely say that, as compared with the competent ecologist of the present day, Boone saw only the surface of things. The incredible intricacies of the plant and animal community—the intrinsic beauty of the organism called America, then in the full bloom of her maidenhood—were as invisible and incomprehensible to Daniel Boone as they are today to Babbitt. The only true development in American recreational resources is the development of the perceptive faculty in Americans. All of the other acts we grace by that name are, at best, attempts to retard or mask the process of dilution.

Let no man jump to the conclusion that Babbitt must take his Ph.D. in ecology before he can 'see' his country. On the contrary, the Ph.D. may become as

callous as an undertaker to the mysteries at which he
officiates. Like all real treasures of the mind, perception can be split into infinitely small fractions without losing its quality. The weeds in a city lot convey
the same lesson as the redwoods; the farmer may see
in his cow-pasture what may not be vouchsafed to the
scientist adventuring in the South Seas. Perception,
in short, cannot be purchased with either learned
degrees or dollars; it grows at home as well as abroad,
and he who has a little may use it to as good advantage as he who has much. As a search for perception, the recreational stampede is footless and unnecessary.

There is, lastly, a fifth component: the sense of
husbandry. It is unknown to the outdoorsman who
works for conservation with his vote rather than with

his hands. It is realized only when some art of management is applied to land by some person of perception. That is to say, its enjoyment is reserved for landholders too poor to buy their sport, and land administrators with a sharp eye and an ecological mind. The tourist who buys access to his scenery misses it altogether; so also the sportsman who hires the state, or some underling, to be his gamekeeper. The Government, which essays to substitute public for private operation of recreational lands, is unwittingly giving away to its field officers a large share of what it seeks to offer its citizens. We foresters and game managers might logically pay for, instead of being paid for, our job as husbandmen of wild crops.

That a sense of husbandry exercised in the production of crops may be quite as important as the crops themselves is realized to some extent in agriculture, but not in conservation. American sportsmen hold in small esteem the intensive game-cropping of the Scottish moors and the German forests, and in some respects rightly. But they overlook entirely the sense of husbandry developed by the European landholder in the process of cropping. We have no such thing as yet. It is important. When we conclude that we must bait the farmer with subsidies to induce him to raise a forest, or with gate receipts to induce him to raise game, we are merely admitting that the pleasures of husbandry-in-the-wild are as yet unknown both to the farmer and to ourselves.

Scientists have an epigram: ontogeny repeats phylogeny. What they mean is that the development of each individual repeats the evolutionary history of the race. This is true of mental as well as physical things. The trophy-hunter is the caveman reborn. Trophy-hunting is the prerogative of youth, racial or individual, and nothing to apologize for.

The disquieting thing in the modern picture is the trophy-hunter who never grows up, in whom the capacity for isolation, perception, and husbandry is undeveloped, or perhaps lost. He is the motorized ant who swarms the continents before learning to see his own back yard, who consumes but never creates outdoor satisfactions. For him the recreational engineer dilutes the wilderness and artificializes its trophies in the fond belief that he is rendering a public service.

The trophy-recreationist has peculiarities that contribute in subtle ways to his own undoing. To enjoy he must possess, invade, appropriate. Hence the wilderness that he cannot personally see has no value to him. Hence the universal assumption that an unused hinterland is rendering no service to society. To those devoid of imagination, a blank place on the map is a useless waste; to others, the most valuable part. (Is my share in Alaska worthless to me because I shall never go there? Do I need a road to show me the arctic prairies, the goose pastures of the Yukon, the Kodiak bear, the sheep meadows behind McKinley?)

It would appear, in short, that the rudimentary grades of outdoor recreation consume their resource-base; the higher grades, at least to a degree, create their own satisfactions with little or no attrition of land or life. It is the expansion of transport without a corresponding growth of perception that threatens us with qualitative bankruptcy of the recreational process. Recreational development is a job not of building roads into lovely country, but of building receptivity into the still unlovely human mind.

The spiritual geography of the western world

MAN IN THE LANDSCAPE

Paul Shepard

A fresh conception of man's place in nature, and how he has looked upon his environment over the ages. *Man in the Landscape* looks through our eyes at the world, and in discovering what we see, tells us what we are.

To order by mail, send $1.25 per book plus 25¢ per order for handling to Ballantine Cash Sales, P.O. Box 505, Westminster, Maryland 21157. Please allow three weeks for handling.

The Publishers Who Brought You Aldo Leopold's
A Sand County Almanac and Edward Abbey's
Desert Solitaire Now Bring You

THE OUTERMOST HOUSE

by
Henry Beston

For more than forty years, this chronicle of a solitary year spent on a Cape Cod beach has remained a classic of nature writing. Written in longhand on a kitchen table, it tells of the ceaseless rhythms of wind, sand, and ocean, the migrations of birds—the natural ebb and flow of a passing year.

A Style of Life Book